My Weekly Word Devotional

TERRANCE KUHN

Published by:
Christian International
177 Apostles Way
Santa Rosa Beach, FL 32459
www.christianinternational.com

In Partnership with:
A Book's Mind
PO Box 272847
Fort Collins, CO 80527
www.abooksmind.com

Copyright © 2014
ISBN: 978-1-939828-61-3
Printed in the United States of America

All scripture quotations are from The Hebrew-Greek Key Word Study Bible, New American Standard Bible, AMG Publishers, c 1984, 1990, 2008 or from the New King James Version (NKJV), Thomas Nelson Publishers, c 1982, Nashville, Tn., USA

Hebrew-Greek word definitions from James Strong's Exhaustive Concordance of the Bible

Foreword
By: Dr. M. Leon Walters

I want to congratulate my friend, co-laborer in Christ and a spiritual son in the Lord, for this most commendable book "My Weekly Word Devotional." Terrance Kuhn has not only given us a weekly devotional but a quick reference dictionary to a wide variety of topics that all of us should review more than once in the course of a year. The author's revelation on each topic is scripturally and doctrinally sound and enlightening for both the new and mature believer.

There are many devotions that will edify. However, this devotional work goes beyond and gives you a library of information based on the word of God that will not only encourage you but lay a foundation with sound doctrine, without compromising the commandments of our Lord.

Terrance, you have done a beautiful job with this book and it will provide the believer with a *Weekly Word Devotional, a Study Guide, a Quick Reference Dictionary* on a wide range of topics that will assist one in *Bible Study, Small Group Discussions, Sermon and Sunday School Preparation as well as personal spiritual growth and understanding of the word of God, with a practical application to one's personal life.*

This should be a desired book for every Christian family's library. I will personally carry a copy of this book in my briefcase as a refresher and quick reference material. Good job Terrance and keep those topical studies coming to the body of Christ.

Blessings As We Read Together
Apostle Dr. M. Leon Walters

Introduction

In today's negative world everyone can use an encouraging word at least once weekly to help them grow in God. The Weekly Word was originally intended for church leaders as an undergirding but then was transformed to encompass all saints of God as all saints are called to be leaders in the Kingdom of God. The Weekly Word is designed to give the reader ample opportunity to not only read, but digest, and be activated in the material presented. Each teaching covers a particular subject with the use of scripture as the basis for each weekly lesson. One may want to read each devotion (teaching) three or four times throughout the week to really absorb the content. There is a column on each page for writing notes and a "seed" prayer at the end of each "word" to begin activating and imparting that particular message into the saint of God. The short prayer is only meant to be a "seed" for the reader to enlarge upon as he/she makes her requests known unto God concerning the subject matter.

The Weekly Word gives the conscientious saint of God the opportunity to study a "word" that is "uttered" directly from heaven; which is why there is to be found very little commentary or explanation in the vast majority of messages. This, however, will not be true for those "words" given with a forward looking (prophetic) direction. God desires His people to grow into a perfect man (Eph. 4:13), into a Bride that is *"a glorious church, not having spot, or wrinkle, or any such thing; but that She should be holy and without blemish"* (Eph. 5:27).

When the Lord Jesus ascended into heaven He left five gifts unto men - some as apostles, some as prophets, some as teachers, some as evangelists, and some as shepherds to the flock (see Psa. 68:18). Their responsibility individually and collectively is *"for the perfecting of the saints, for the work of the ministry, for the edifying of the body of Christ"* (Eph. 5:12). No one person can fulfill all of these gifts as only the Lord Jesus could. The different gifts must work together to bring about God's desired result and plan.

Each ascension gift awards its own anointings and focus; the most consolidated gift being the apostle. In many places one may have a shepherd (pastor) watching over their souls but the teaching, the getting into the very minute details of the word to aid the hearer in growing in God, may be missing. Likewise, much of the Church has been void of a prophetic voice to direct the Church and speak holiness into the life. All five of these gifts are necessary for proper spiritual growth.

The Weekly Word is designed to bring the reader *"line upon line and precept upon precept"* (Is. 28:10) into more of the truth, presence, and glory of God in order to impact society and their spheres of influence on a daily basis. The Weekly Word is not intended to replace any other anointed gift that God has placed in the reader's life; merely to aid them in bringing the Body of Christ to a mature Bride for her beloved Bridegroom.

As for use, the Weekly Word would be appropriate not only for individual study but for group study, a weekly Bible study, or church school classes.

The Teacher

A teacher is one who gives instruction from what he has been taught or experienced. This is why it is important to understand that the "teacher" is one of the five ascension gifts, so named because they were given at the time of the ascension of our Lord, and are, in reality, an extension of the ministry of Jesus. Therefore, it must be taken with no minor thought as to what a "teacher" teaches. There are many voices within the Church today that are speaking different messages; enough to confound the hearer. We are told, *"Take care what you listen to. By your standard of measure it shall be measured to you; and more shall be given you besides"* (Mk. 4:24). If a person receives a teaching that is not true, or semi-true; or if one denies a true teaching than the way that person has measured that teaching will be measured to them.

The best way to find if a human teacher is teaching the truth is to find what the number one teacher, the Holy Spirit, is saying. *"But the Comforter, the Holy Spirit, whom the Father will send in My name, He will teach you all things, and bring to your remembrance all that I said to you"* (Jn. 14:26). The initial source of teaching is the Holy Spirit and He does not teach one thing to one person and something opposite to another. At the same time He anoints certain people with the gift of "Teacher" to come alongside those who have another predominant role in bringing the saints to maturity so that in time they might fulfill their proper role in the Church.

A teacher must first hear the truth from the Holy Spirit and then have it confirmed by men led by the Holy Spirit, or, he must have what he hears from men confirmed by the written Word and the Holy Spirit. When Paul, an apostle, speaks of his own calling he says, *"and for this I was appointed a preacher, and an apostle (I am telling the truth, I am not lying) as a teacher of the Gentiles in faith and truth"* (1 Ti. 2:7).

Paul explains his own preparation for ministry in Galatians 1:12-2:1. He begins his dissertation in Galatians 1:11, *"For I would have you know, brethren, that the gospel which was preached by me is not according to man. For I neither received it from man, nor was I taught it, but I received it through a revelation of Jesus Christ."* This sounds reminiscent of the way John received what he taught. Paul ends his dissertation to the Galatians pertaining to his equipping with these words, *"Then after an interval of fourteen years I went up again to Jerusalem with Barnabas, taking Titus along also. And it was because of a revelation that I went up; and I submitted to them the gospel which I preach among the Gentiles, but I did so in private to those of reputation, for fear that I might be running, or had run, in vain."*

The Weekly Word was begun in April, 2011 and was sent to over seventy leaders and leaders-in-training. Some of those are apostles, prophets, evangelists, shepherds, and teachers; so these "words" have been presented to and affirmed by many appointed gifts to the body.

The Prophetic

This gift actually has three different distinctions within it. There is the spirit of prophecy spoken of in Revelation 19:10, *"For the testimony of Jesus is the spirit of prophecy."* The word testimony means "evidence given" and includes any truth that is spoken about the Lord Jesus concerning His birth, life, death, resurrection, or future events including the marriage supper of the Lamb.

The second level is the gift of prophecy spoken of in 1 Corinthians 14:1-3, *"Pursue love, yet desire earnestly spiritual gifts, that especially that you may prophesy. For one who speaks in a tongue <u>does not speak to men, but to God</u>; for no one understands, but in his spirit he speaks mysteries. But one who prophesies speaks to men for edification and exhortation and consolation"* (underlining authors). The gift of prophecy, which is given to us by the Holy Spirit, is to edify, exhort, and comfort the individual receiving the prophecy.

The third level of prophetic ministry is the gift of Prophet that is given to the Body of Christ by Jesus Christ. Ephesians 4:10-11, *"He who descended is Himself also He who ascended far above all the heavens, that He might fill all things. And He gave some as apostles, and some as prophets, and some as evangelists, and some as pastors and teachers, for the equipping of the saints for the work of service, to the building up of the Body of Christ; until we all attain to the unity of the faith, and of the knowledge of the Son of God, to a mature man, to the measure of the stature which belongs to the fullness of Christ."* Throughout history the Prophet has been used to rebuke, direct, council, and speak words of comfort and judgment to others.

The Weekly Word - Week 1

Repent

When John the Baptist came preaching in the wilderness he said, *"Repent, for the Kingdom of heaven is at hand"* (Mat. 3:2). When the Lord Jesus began to preach He also said, *"The time is fulfilled, and the Kingdom of God is at hand. Repent and believe in the gospel"* (Mk. 1:15). Both John the Baptist and the Lord Jesus Christ commanded men to repent for their sins and then to focus on, to set their eyes upon, the Kingdom that is beyond this world. Not only did both of them preach that men should repent from dead works (religious deeds) but they began to impart a new vision to those who heard their voice, *"For the Kingdom of heaven is at hand.* The Lord Jesus and John the Baptist both preached that there was a better life on the other side of repentance.

Preaching repentance from sin and dead works and looking unto the Kingdom of God has widely been replaced by the preaching of faith. Faith toward God is a necessity but cannot replace the preaching of repentance and looking to the Kingdom. Faith can only be added to it. The preaching of repentance begins with the evangelistic spirit and continues with the apostolic teaching as we find in the epistles written by Paul.

The unbeliever (sinner) must understand that his or her lifestyle is not acceptable in the eyes of God and even the life of a believer (saint) must be set on the highway of holiness. *"The highway of the upright is to depart from evil, he who keeps his way preserves his* soul" (Pro. 16:17).

God has prepared a road, a highway for the people of God to travel upon and it is not a dusty, dung covered road of ancient days. *"A highway shall be there, and a road, and it shall be called the Highway of Holiness. The unclean shall not pass*

*over it, but it shall be for others. Whoever walks the road, al-
though a fool, shall not go astray"* (Is. 35:8).

Paul lists the works of the flesh in his letter to the Ephesians,
scolds Corinth for being divisive, presents a list of fleshly sins
to both the Colossians and the Galatians, and encourages the
Philippians to be of one accord. If one is continuing to preach
against the sins of the flesh as well as laying a foundation of
faith toward God, not only for initial salvation but for spiritual
growth, that person is to be commended and deserves double
honor. The Lord Jesus commanded His disciples, *"Go therefore and make disciples of all the nations, baptizing them in the
name (authority and character) of the Father and of the Son
and the Holy Spirit, teaching them to observe all that I have
commanded you"* (Mat. 28:18; parenthesis mine). The word
"observe" means to "watch, guard against loss or injury, or to
keep the eye upon".

As we gaze at many segments of Christendom we can see
that they have not laid hold of what Jesus taught but what man
has substituted. Many churches no longer preach repentance as
a foundational truth. Both John the Baptist and the Lord Jesus
said to focus on the Kingdom after one repented. We are not
to focus on our deficiencies but on the purity of Christ, our example. By not focusing correctly much sin has been allowed
to destroy many lives within the Church. Many surveys have
been completed which have shown that way too many ministers, church leaders, and saints, are living in sin and have a weak
attitude towards sin.

As the newborn saint is taught to *"seek first the Kingdom
of God and His righteousness"* (Mat. 6:19) he can grow in the
truths of the Lord. The righteousness, peace, and joy in the
Holy Spirit, comprising the Kingdom of God, will be his/hers.
The Kingdom of God is only found in the Holy Spirit. The Lord
Jesus told the Pharisees that the Kingdom of God does not come
with observation but is within a person.

Prayer: *Father, please help me to repent of my sins and help
me to enter into the Kingdom of God.*

The Weekly Word - Week 2
Maturity

The Church of the Living God is expected to search out and to perform the works of God that were manifested by the Lord Himself. Psalm 111:2 reads, *"The works of the LORD are great, sought out by all them that have pleasure therein."* A survey of what this verse is actually saying reveals a great deal. Looking at what the Hebrew originally says it would read, "The actions of the LORD are great, followed or frequented of all them that have desire or see value therein."

The Church today must be inclined, or desire, to once again see the works of God performed; she must find value in them once again. The Church must consider the works of God to be of great value and must desire to once again be ignited by the Holy Spirit to perform His works. The Church has gone through almost 50 years since the last "pouring out" of His Spirit. God is preparing to "pour out" His Spirit afresh and in a mighty way and the Church must be ready to receive Him. Those who do not acknowledge this pouring out (spoken of in Acts 2) will find themselves on the wrong side of history. The question is "Who is on the Lord's side?"

The little trickle of anointing that we have experienced in the past years, which has been nothing more than a slowly flowing brook, will soon become a mighty rushing river of the Holy Spirit destroying the things that are of the earth in our lives and cleansing us for service unto Him.

In the Tabernacle of Moses the priest had to wash himself before entering the second, or inner, court to give service unto the LORD. This is what God will do in this outpouring. No longer will dirty vessels be allowed to serve Him. No longer will we watch as the waves of the Spirit gently caress the sandy seashore. We are about to observe God pouring out His Spirit upon all flesh, the saint and the sinner, and all will be convicted of sin, righteousness, and justice. His sons and His daughters will prophesy, experience visions and dreams, heal the sick, cast out devils, and work mighty wonders. This will be the portion of the saints.

The day is on the horizon when a church will no longer need to send for a prophet, or an evangelist working miracles, for God is going to do a new thing. He is going to visit His people and equip every saint who believes with the power from on high. Yes, God will still work through His ascension gifts to perfect the saints and equip the saints but the struggle will be removed.

The day is soon coming where we will see the manifestation of Hebrews 8:11, "None *of them shall teach His neighbor and none His brother, saying, 'Know the Lord' for all shall know Me, from the least to the greatest of them.*" The day of a weak, immature Church is coming to an end and the day of the full grown mature woman Church is near. The Lord Jesus gave us this promise "*Surely, surely I say unto you, he that believes on Me, the works that I do shall he do also; and greater works than these shall he do; because I go unto My Father*" (Jn. 14:12). The Lord Jesus promises us that if we have faith in Him than we will be equipped to do greater works than what He did. Jesus had compassion on the sick and healed, He cast out devils, He raised the dead, and He walked on water. All while preaching the Kingdom of God.

In the book of Daniel we find these words, "*And such as do wickedly against the covenant shall he (king of the south) corrupt by flatteries: but the people who do know their God shall be strong and do exploits*" (11:32). Those who acknowledge their God will be courageous as Joshua and war against the enemies of sickness, demonic oppression, and death. This is the portion for the Church as she matures before the Lord.

Prayer: *Father, I want to mature and become the saint of God that you have purposed me to be even before the foundation of the earth. I desire to perform the works you have called me to perform in your name.*

The Weekly Word - Week 3
We are of Value to God

While sitting in church one Sunday the Lord brought to mind Matthew 6:26. What the Lord spoke to me had nothing to do with what was being spoken of and I instantly knew what God was up to - "The Weekly Word". Matthew 6:26 says, *"Look at the birds of the air, for they neither sow nor reap nor gather into barns; yet your heavenly Father feeds them. Are you not of more value than they?"* The answer is "Yes, we are!" Why are we of value to the Lord?

1. It is through us that God will judge the world. When Paul is arguing against the saints in Corinth for going to law for judgment he writes, *"Do you not know that the saints will judge the world? And if the world will be judged by you, are you unworthy to judge the smallest matters?* (I Cor. 6:2) The saints are called upon by God to judge the world. Not only in the last day but as we walk on the earth today. We are to be in the world but not of the world and we are to judge the world as sinful. If the saints of God do not judge (consider) the world to be sinful they will partake of it and no longer be salt or light.

2. It is for us that Christ died. Enough said.

3. We are His family. *"For as many as are led by the Spirit of God, these are sons (daughters) of God"* (Rom. 8:14). We are not only friends; we are sons and daughters to God and brothers and sisters to Jesus (Rom. 8:29). Hebrews 2:10 - *"For it was fitting for Him (our Father), for whom are all things, and by whom are all things, in bringing many sons to glory, to make the captain of our salvation (Jesus) perfect through suffering."*

4. We are predestined to a purpose - "*In Him also we have obtained an inheritance, being predestined according to the purpose of Him who works all things according to the counsel of His will*" (Eph. 1:11). Each one of us is called according to His will to do His purpose - to destroy the works of the evil one. Also Eph. 1:4, "*just as He chose us in Him before the foundation of the world, that we should be holy and without blame before Him in love.*"

5. We are to rule over nations with Him. "*And he who overcomes, and keeps My works until the end, to him I will give power over the nations - He shall rule them with a rod of iron; they shall be dashed to pieces like the potters vessels*" (Rev. 2:26-27).

6. We are to give Him glory - "*Let them give glory to the LORD, and declare His praise in the coastlands*" (Is. 42:12).

These are only a few of the reasons that we are of great value to the Lord. There are many more.

Prayer: *Father God, let me understand the value that I have in your eyes that I may begin to see myself the way you see me.*

The Weekly Word - Week 4
Desire Spiritual Gifts

If a person really desires to operate in signs, wondrous works, and the gifts of the Holy Spirit there a few actions one can take to achieve the desired goal. We in the 21st century have been taught all about faith and how by faith we can achieve a great deal. But as we come closer to the final day God is requiring more of His people.

The apostle Paul wrote that we should desire spiritual gifts (1 Cor. 14:1). We are told to long for, crave, covet, yearn, hunger after, or lust for spiritual gifts. The works of God do not come to one having only a lukewarm desire for them. When a person wants a certain size house or an expensive automobile he will do what it takes to earn the means to purchase it. When a man finds a woman he wants to marry he will do what it takes to win her affections. If a person wants a promotion he/she will do what it takes to acquire the qualifications necessary. The idea is that the required action will be taken to receive the desired result.

Let us look at just four principles that a person could utilize to move in signs, wondrous works, and the gifts of the Holy Spirit. First, we must always be cognizant of our weaknesses toward sin. This keeps us humble so as not to think of ourselves more highly than what we ought to think. We may have defeated sin in many areas of our lives but we must be alert less we be blindsided by something we thought we had overcome. We are called to be overcomers; overcomers of sin and overcomers of the world. We must keep a mindset of being victorious and not defeated. If we need to repent for something done or neglected we must repent and make it right with God.

Second, if we desire to do the works of God than we will pray for them, remember the works of old, meditate on them, and talk about them to ourselves or to our fellow servants. The psalmist writes, "*Sing to Him, sing psalms to Him, and talk of all His wondrous works*" (1 Chr. 16:9). The word "talk" means to ponder, converse, or utter. It means to converse with one-self aloud or to pray to the Lord. 1 Chronicles 16:24 tells us, "*Declare His glory among the nations, His wonders among all peoples.*" "Declare" means "to tally, or enumerate, to recount or celebrate". The Church today constantly recounts the death and resurrection of Jesus but we must also celebrate His wondrous works. The psalmist Asaph wrote, "*I will remember the works of the LORD; surely I will remember your wonders of old*" (Ps. 77:11). When Asaph speaks of how he will remember the works of God he is saying he will talk to others about them. The apostle Paul wrote "*be filled with the Spirit, speaking to one another in psalms and hymns and spiritual songs, singing and making melody in your heart to the Lord, giving thanks always for all things to God the Father in the name of our Lord Jesus Christ*" (Eph.5:18-20).

The third attribute we must grow in, or unlock, is compassion for the sick, possessed, and unfortunate. "*And Jesus went forth and saw a great multitude, and was moved with compassion toward them, and He healed their sick*" (Mat 14:14). Jesus healed out of compassion and we must also.

The fourth action is faith. We must move out of faith and we must move in faith knowing that the Lord desires all to be healed just as He desires all to be saved. Jesus never turned a sick person away. He healed them all.

Prayer: *Lord Jesus, I desire to move in the gifts of the Holy Spirit to edify the Body of Christ and to glorify Your name. I ask that You give me those gifts that You have purposed for me to move in to minister to the unsaved. I ask that You stir up the compassion that You have placed within me to heal the sick, cast out demons, and raise the dead.*

The Weekly Word - Week 5
Fulfilling Your Place

It is commonly understood that those who are called into an ascension gift ministry have the primary responsibility of equipping the members of the Body of Christ to perform his/her membership ministry so that the whole Body of Christ may become a *"perfect man, to the measure of the stature of the fullness of Christ"* (Eph.4:13). No one person can become equal to this stature alone. It must be accomplished as a body of believers. No one local assembly can accomplish this alone. It must be done with the rest of the Body of Christ. Speaking of the prophets that came before us the writer of Hebrews relates, *"And all these having obtained a good testimony through faith, did not receive the promise, God having provided something better for us, that they should not be made perfect apart from us"* (Heb. 11:39-40). All those that are in Christ must come into their proper place to fulfill their proper function in order for the Body of Christ to be mature.

So how does each person know, or find, the part of the Body in which they are to dwell? Does each person need to wait until they are prophesied over? Does each person need to wait until his or her shepherd designates them for a certain position? Does each person just sit in the audience of a church waiting for a lightning bolt to come out of the clear blue sky, hitting them on the head, or an angel to drop a note in their lap? Every person when they are born again receives a call on their life for some ministry to the Body. In Proverbs 6 we read, *"Go to the ant, you sluggard! Consider her ways and be wise, which, having no captain, overseer or ruler, provides her supplies in the summer, and gathers her food in the harvest. How long will you slumber, O sluggard? When will you rise from your sleep?"* (6-9)

The point of this verse is not that she stores in the summer but that she goes about performing the task that is necessary for her to accomplish; that has been put in her by God. Every local church has parts of the Body of Christ within it that are listening to be readied, hoping to be recognized, or waiting to be released. It is the responsibility of the leaders and the individual to work together to bring the call and anointing to fruition.

When a person is first born again he/she must be readied. Each person may become prepared for service in a different time frame than others and the leaders must be looking for the proper amount of time to pass for each individual. During this time they must be actively equipping the saint for service.

Some people think they need less time than they actually do in order to perform properly. Others are happy to just sit and pickle while God is saying, "It is time." Some people sit in the audience of a church hoping to be recognized but the leader is too busy, or too blind, to see the hand of God on the individual's life. Others are cast out because the leader(s) see the call on the life and become jealous or afraid, refusing to give place to the call. At other times the background of a leader may interfere with the recognition of an anointing. If the leader does not believe that apostles and prophets are still in operation today than they will think someone is called to be a pastor or teacher and cause much stress in the relationship.

Once the gift is recognized the leaders and the individual must work together towards a time of release. If one is endowed with one of the nine gifts of the Holy Ghost encouragement must be given to the person to operate in that gift within the Body to build confidence. The person must be encouraged to stir up the gift as Paul encouraged Timothy, not suppressed to keep it hidden. If a person believes he/she has a ministry outside the walls of the church that must be pursued and they must be equipped and encouraged to go forth. As the ant, God has at least one gift in each person's spirit. It must be stirred up and released.

Prayer: *Lord Jesus, I ask that You inform me as to what I need to do to move into my proper place in Your Body. I no longer want to just be part of an audience. I want to be activated in the place of service that You want me to fulfill. Also, Lord Jesus, I ask that You bring the proper leaders into my life to set me in place as You would desire.*

The Weekly Word - Week 6
Be A Friend To Your Leaders

In over two decades of ministry I have found that the most important aspect of a minister's life is relationship. I am talking about having a close relationship with others that will help keep one another steady and on course for what God desires. The Lord Jesus had a close relationship with the twelve disciples, in addition to the women who followed Him and ministered to Him (Mat. 27:55). While teaching these disciples and imparting Himself unto them He also allowed them to become intimate friends with Him and partake of His joys and His sorrows (Mat. 10:5-8; Lk 10:1). For instance, He told them what was going to happen to Him so that they would not become discouraged and fall away (Mat. 16:21). In the upper room there were 120 disciples who did as He commanded, to wait for the glory of God to come. After being together for 40 days these disciples were not only close to Jesus, but to one another. They were in unity.

Maranathalife.com has done a survey concerning the lives of pastors. Here are some of the results. "Fifteen hundred pastors leave the ministry each month due to moral failures, spiritual burnout or contention in their churches. Four thousand new churches begin each year, but over seven thousand churches close. Fifty percent of pastors' marriages end in divorce. Eighty percent of pastors and 84% of their spouses feel unqualified and discouraged in their role as pastors. Fifty percent of pastors are so discouraged that they would leave the ministry if they could, but have no other way of making a living. Eighty percent of seminary and Bible school graduates who enter the ministry will leave the ministry within the first five years."

These are startling statistics and it is the view of this writer, and others, that the number one cure for this widespread catastrophe is "RELATIONSHIP". All church leaders need close friends, confidants, and mentors who live in the body and who edify and encourage them steadily. Ministers need to have those of equal stature, greater stature, and lesser stature, who they can confide in and share their secrets. Jesus was close to those who were His followers and leaders need those relationships also.

Each church leader has a specific gifting and calling, anointing, from the Lord. One leader does not minister the same way as another leader does, even if they have the same gifting. There are differences in administrations. Nor does one prophet minister the same way as another prophet does. All ascension gifts are focused on bringing the Body of Christ to perfection. Each part of the body needs the several gifts that Jesus endowed her with. Church leaders need to be in close association with other church leaders receiving them as friends and brothers and sisters in Christ instead of through a lens of distrust, suspicion, and competition.

A minister may have a close associate who is under the same roof, i.e. in the same ministry, yet there may not be that ability, or freedom, to share the most inward thoughts. Having relationships outside of those walls will aid the hurting. Leaders need not go through life alone. Leaders need to reach out and build relationships. God will build and bless these relationships.

Prayer: *Father, I ask, Lord, that you allow me to be a strong companion to those You have set in place to guide my life; that they can confide in me and I will not abandon that confidence; that they would experience the love and gratitude that I have for them so that they would be comfortable in all that they do.*

The Weekly Word - Week 7
Accomplishment

A main reason leaders need to have relationships with others of like passion is to enable each one to have the possibility of fulfilling one's destiny. Servants of God are able to encourage and build up one another in the fear of the Lord and to help each other continue to pursue the prize that is set before him/her. Every believer should desire to hear the words, "Well done, good and faithful servant" as he/she enters into eternity. Many times depression, discouragement, distractions, or disease will bring detriment to one's destiny. As the servants of God join together they can aid one another in the continual pursuit of accomplishing the tasks God has given each one to perform.

The word "tasks" is used above because few leaders are given only one task. To look at it another way, a general task may have several smaller tasks which must be accomplished to finish the larger task. The apostle Paul instructs us that "*he who plows should plow in hope*" (1 Cor. 9:10). The laborer must continue to labor until the seed that is sown comes to harvest. The words of Jesus tell us that He desires to find His servants doing their assignments when He returns (Mat 24:46). When a farmer plows a field and sows seed he does so with the hope of receiving back a favorable harvest. He plows in order to break up the fallow ground, removing rocks, and uprooting weeds that are living on the land. After plowing, he sows in hope for a favorable harvest.

The major task of bringing forth a good harvest includes plowing, sowing, weeding, eliminating the rocks and thistles, and amending the soil so as to have the correct balance of ph and nutrients. Many churches have a ground of clay, sand, or silt. Each one of these types must be amended with other types of soil. We are told that it is important to have the elements of faith, hope, and love in our lives. These three must be balanced correctly to create the proper soil.

The Lord Jesus tells us in Luke 9:62, *"No one, having put his hand to the plow, and looking back, is fit for the kingdom of God."* In context, the Lord Jesus is referring to those whom He calls to Himself but worldly distractions deter them from properly performing their assigned task. Remember how that Lot's wife looked back at Sodom as God destroyed it, not to see what was happening, but because she had found pleasure in Sodom, she cared about Sodom, a city of wickedness. A farmer, while in the midst of working his field must not look back with pleasure at what he has already accomplished as if to say, "Look what I have achieved" but must continue forward until all of the land that has been entrusted to him produces a large harvest. It is not what has already been accomplished that is as important but what is yet to be accomplished.

Prayer: *Father, help me to keep my eyes on the task at hand that it might be fully accomplished, bringing forth a great harvest, in due season.*

The Weekly Word - Week 8
Hope

We are told in 1 Corinthians 13:13 that there are three qualities that abide within us to keep us secure in Christ - faith, hope, love. Usually when there is a list of subjects written in the Word of God there is a progression to it whether it be from greatest to least or from increasing to decreasing order. We are told, by Paul, that of these three the greatest is love. So, love is seen here as being greater than faith. What about hope, is it greater than faith? The writer of the epistle to the Hebrews writes, "Now faith is the substance of things hoped for, the evidence of things not seen" (11:1). Defining this sentence we may read, "Now our persuasion is the under support of things expected or anticipated." Abraham found the importance of hope when he walked in the personal prophetic word (rhema) spoken to him by God, "*who, contrary to hope, in hope believed, so that he became the father of many nations, according to what was spoken,*" (Rom. 4:18). For Abraham to grasp the fulfillment of the rhema word spoken to him by God he needed to operate in hope.

For every saint of God, it is imperative that he/she operates in hope. Hope does not come automatically, it is developed, as Paul states, "*tribulation produces perseverance and perseverance character, and character, hope*" (R0m. 5:3-4). Hope is produced by having character, the character of the Lord Jesus Christ within us (Col. 1:27). Faith does not have a direction without hope; having an understanding of what to envision.

There is also a great connection between faith and hope. "*For we through the Spirit eagerly wait for the hope of righteousness by faith*" (Gal. 5:5). We come unto salvation through justification by faith and in this passage Paul is saying that it is through the Spirit, not the law that we hope for this justification. So we find that hope works with faith to bring forth the desired result. We also find that God is the origin of our hope. He ini-tiates hope, *"Now may the God of hope fill you with all joy and peace in believing, that you may abound in hope by the power of the Holy Spirit"* (Rom. 15:13). We abound, grow, in hope through the power of the Holy Ghost. Now, much of what Paul writes about hope concerns initial salvation and having hope in Christ or the hope that we have laid up in heaven (Col.1:5). But hope can strengthen us to press on.

In the final analysis we find that the Lord Jesus Christ is our hope (1 Tim 1:1). If we find that if our hope for anything is out-side the will of God we will find ourselves to be most miserable. But since our hope is in Him we need not fear that whatever He has spoken will not come to pass as it was with Abraham, Isaac, and Jacob. Whether God speaks to us through an impression, whisper, or audible voice, or He speaks to us through a prophet or prophetic person concerning our destiny we can put hope in those words even if they be delayed. It is a true statement that, *"Hope deferred makes the heart sick, but when the desire comes it is a tree of life"* (Pro. 13:12).

When God puts His desire for our lives into our hearts He starts, as it were, with a faint echo or pull. He then begins to form that desire so that we can begin to grasp what it is He wants. He then increases our desire to see it come to pass in our lives and in His timing He will bring it forth as a woman in labor. It may not always be hard labor but it will come forth in a way that other people know it has been birthed.

Prayer: *Father God, I ask that You stir up faith, hope, and love within me so that I might walk a life in Christ that is worthy of You.*

The Weekly Word - Week 9
Dispersing The Wine

The Word of God tells us that we can't put new wine into old bottles, or wineskins. A wine skin is a container that holds the wine and keeps the wine fresh until it is needed, within a certain time frame. In the first century New Testament Church the wineskin could become hard and break or crack when it became old, thus, allowing the wine to pour out onto the ground and be wasted. In order for the wine to stay fresh and the wine skin to stay usable the wine had to be dispensed in a suitable amount of time or the wineskin would stretch or become brittle.

We all have seen saints of God who have sat in the audience and done nothing with the new wine that has been poured into them with the Holy Ghost (sacred breath) of God. If we consider ourselves as being the wineskin that dispenses the New Wine to others, and we keep the new wine to ourselves than we as individuals are likely to become brittle and of no good use. As the Lord pours in the wine we must allow it to go forth to those around us and not hold it within. As the individual saint disperses New Wine to the world he infects with the light of God he can be refilled with yet a Newer Wine as the Lord continues to pour in this Wine.

The apostle John wrote concerning Jesus, "*He who believes in Me, as the Scripture has said, out of his heart will flow rivers of living water*" (Jn 7:38). John 7:39 explains that Jesus was speaking concerning the Holy Ghost. Jesus says that we must believe in Him as the Scripture says, not just any way we want to believe. We must believe that He is the risen Christ, not just a buried man who spoke a good word. We must believe that He is our strength, our song, our high tower, our fortress, our healer, our deliverer from evil oppression, our bulwark, our advocate, our mediator, and our hope.

We must also understand that He is still on a mission. In the Revelation of Jesus Christ the angel describes the one hundred and forty-four thousand in part, *"These are the ones who follow the Lamb wherever He goes. These were redeemed from among men, being firstfruits to God and to the Lamb"* (Rev 14:4). So where is the Lamb going? The word "goes" actually is interpreted to "lead from underneath". The Lamb of God is leading His Bride to her destination by being an undergirding force. He holds us up even in the midst of our greatest trials and fights with the powers and principalities that war against our minds.

During the past five hundred years Jesus has been leading His Church from glory to glory as She begins to adorn herself for the wedding. He started with justification by faith, baptism, the renewal of the Baptism with the Holy Ghost and fire, the call to holiness, the reinstitution of the five ascension gifts of pastor, teacher, evangelist, prophet, and apostle, and now He is putting His fiery presence in each individual saint. Each saint must allow this new wine of the Spirit to flow from his heart on a daily basis, thereby being renewed and refreshed at all times.

Prayer*: Father fill me anew with your New Wine that I may be refreshed and can be poured out unto others,*

The Weekly Word - Week 10
The Death of Compromise

There is a new paradigm shift coming to the Body of Christ and this shift will change the way the Church looks at the world. The Church must begin to view the world the way that Jesus truly views the world. First, He sees the world clothed in sin. He sees His Body, the Church, clothed in righteousness. He sees the world as totally in rebellion against His word, will, and way. He sees His Church in partial obedience to His word, will, and way.

The Church today is following the same course of action as did the Israelites when they fought against the six tribes that inhabited Canaan - the Canaanites, the Hittites, the Amorites, the Hivites, the Perizzites, and the Jebusites. By definition the Canaanites were wondering peddlers, the Amorites dwelt in the mountains, the Perizzites dwelt in the open country, and the Hivites dwelt in villages. Thus, we see that Israel was to conquer every type of land and people. But Joshua 13 informs us that not all of the land was taken and because of this failure these peoples began to intermarry with the sons and daughters of Israel causing them to follow after idols.

Today the Church of the Living God dwells among false religions and people who hate God, and His Church. Just as the Canaanites, Hittites, Amorites, Hivites, Perizzites, and Jebusites hated the Israelites because they served the true God, so the cities that we dwell in hate us because of the God we serve. They exist alongside of us only because we have not been a loud voice, as John the Baptist, the leaders of the Protestant reformation, or our Lord has been in the past.

Our fear of persecution and suffering has quieted our voice to a whisper. But we are told by our Lord to *"Preach the gospel to every creature"* (Mk. 16:15). We are to herald, be a public crier, the gospel of Jesus Christ before the heathen. *"There-fore I will give thanks to you, O LORD, among the heathen (gentiles, uncircumcised), and sing praises to your name"* (Ps. 18:49). The Lord does not just want us to proclaim His name in the sanctuary; He wants us to do it in the public square, in pa-rades, and on the streets. *"Go out into the highways and hedges, and compel them to come in, that My house may be filled"* (Lk 14:23). It is obvious that most sinners would rather serve an-other Christ than the one that died on the cross. Not that there is another Christ but they have manufactured one in their minds and so has the Church of the living God to some extent.

For instance, we are seeing many winds and rain upon the land these days. Some say the wind is from the Lord, some say it is from the devil. In researching the word of God there is not one scripture that tells us that the devil sends the wind. However, there are many that say the LORD sends the wind. *"And Moses stretched out his hand over the sea; and the LORD caused the sea to go back by a strong east wind all that night ..."* (Ex 14:21). In Genesis 41 we see where Pharaoh dreamed two dreams. In the second dream the ears of corn were blasted by the east wind. In these dreams God was not prophesying what the devil was going to do but what He was going to do. The LORD is in charge of the wind. *"For He commands and raises the stormy wind, which lifts up the waves of the sea"* (Ps. 107:25). Psalm 148:8 reads, *"Fire and hail, snow and clouds, stormy wind fulfilling His word."* The false church and the world would have us believe that God could not send a storm that would destroy lives and buildings but that it is contrary to His word.

There are two venues that God is going to use in this new paradigm - outdoor preaching, and preaching within the false churches that we live among. On Sunday the largest place one can find lost souls is in false churches, or at a ballgame. God is going to send His servants, two by two, into these enclaves to preach His word. These saints will not necessarily be full-time ministers - just those He appoints and sends. God is stirring the waters to no longer allow His Church to live peacefully along-side the heathen of this world. He desires lost souls to be saved and He will use His Church to do it as the Holy Spirit blows His wind upon Her.

Prayer: *Lord, I don't want You to see me as one who com-promises with the world. Bring to my attention any thought or action that You see as a compromise in my life and take it from me so that I can be holy in Your sight.*

.

.

The Weekly Word - Week 11
The Flesh

Matthew 10:38-39 says, *"And he who does not take his cross and follow after Me is not worthy of Me. He who finds his life will lose it, and he who loses his life for My sake will find it."* In these two verses we find the heart of being a servant of God, a follower of Christ. To bear our cross means to lose our life. "Our life" is identical to the works of the flesh.

A second hidden aspect in this statement appears when we turn the words spoken by Jesus inside out. If a person who does not take his cross and follow after Jesus is seen as unworthy than a person who takes up his cross and follows after Jesus is worthy of Him. The Lord Jess set the standard by saying to us "If you do not take up your cross and follow me you are then unworthy of me". Those who are seen as unworthy of Jesus do not follow Jesus. By setting these parameters Jesus is saying that those who follow Him are worthy of Him.

When the Lord Jesus was placed on the cross the one thing that died on that cross was His flesh. As we bear our cross and follow Jesus the one thing that will die is our flesh. But our flesh will not die unless we follow Jesus. This does not mean to merely acknowledge Him as Savior but to follow Him wherever He goes. Where is He leading you at this time? Is He leading you to spend more time in prayer or in His word? Is He leading you to seek out additional avenues of becoming equipped for His service beyond just the local assembly? Is He tugging at your heart to become more intimate with Him?

When the children of Israel walked through the wilderness for forty years they would walk for a while and then camp, walk for a while and then camp. Every time they walked or camped, they learned something new about God or saw some new spiritual truth surrounding God. The forty years in the wilderness was not just a time of punishment. It was a time of learning. It was a time of learning to follow and trust in the LORD. *"When-ever the cloud was taken up from above the tabernacle, the chil-dren of Israel would go forward in all their journeys. But if the cloud was not taken up, then they did not journey till the day that it was taken up"* (Ex. 40:36-37). No matter how many churches or denominations man has started God still only sees one Church, He only sees one Bride. The Body of Christ, as fractured as it is by the moving in the flesh, must come together into the unity that Christ prayed for us to come into in John 17.

We must realize that there is only one Church of Jesus Christ and He has one vision for His Bride - for her to come into per-fection. In the garden of Gethsemane, where Jesus went many times to pray, in His final prayer Jesus prayed, *"O My Father, if it is possible, let this cup pass from Me; nevertheless, not as I will, but as You will"* (Mat. 26:39). Even after ministering for three years and leading His disciples, teaching them all things regarding the Kingdom, the Lord Jesus goes into the garden and admits that He still must submit His will to His God. When He went to the cross and died to the flesh, was buried, and was resurrected by the power of God He could then breathe on His disciples and say, *"Receive the Holy Spirit"* (John 20:22).

When any saint ministers the breath of God on one who is in need, extending the Spirit of God to that person, they are operating as one with God or nothing would happen. But those times are far too few and far between. The Lord wants His pow-er to be displayed every day of the week on every corner of the city. In some cities there is at least one church on every corner. Why can't the power of God be displayed on every corner? Is it because the Church is divided by vision or will? *"Can two walk together, unless they are agreed?"* (Amos 3:3) *"We will walk in the name of the LORD our God forever and ever"* (Mic. 4:5). Let us walk and build the Kingdom of God together.

Prayer: *Lord, I want to walk in the Spirit of God and not in the flesh. Help me to walk after the things of God and not my own desires. Let me be a source of bringing Your desires to fruition that Your Church would be one.*

The Weekly Word - Week 12
Multi-dimensional Ministries

In 2004 the title of my thesis for my masters from Christian International School of Theology was "A Study of Uni-Dimensional Ministries Versus Multi-Dimensional Ministries". In preparing for this undertaking I was surprised to find the number of voices that were trumpeting the need in the Church for Multi-Dimensional Ministry in the local church. Many of these voices, however, were not voices of those in leadership but those from the pew calling out for completion of the Body of Christ. A second class of these voices was made up of prophetic voices pointing towards where God wanted to take the Church.

Filling the need that the saints have to be fully equipped is not an easy assignment. That is why the Lord has always determined for the ministry to be shared. We see when Jesus sent out His disciples that He sent them two by two. The words of Solomon in Ecclesiastes 4:9-12 explain this, *"Two are better than one because they have a good return for their labor. For if either of them falls, the one will lift up his companion. But woe to the one who falls when there is not another to lift him up. Furthermore, if two lie down together they keep warm, but how can one be warm alone? And if one can overpower him who is alone, two can resist him. A cord of three strands is not quickly torn apart."* When two walk together they add strength to one another. The one who would attack (devil) now needs to try to find a weakness that both share and it becomes harder for the attacker to find a weakness. One being alone is much easier to defeat because when he falls there is no one to lift him up. There is no one for him to receive counsel from or get direction. It is even more powerful to have a "cord of three strands."

This is evident in the events which took place in Antioch of Syria concerning Saul and Barnabus. Saul had been converted on the road to Damascus and is taken by Barnabus to Antioch a city 300 miles north of Jerusalem. God takes this occasion to speak to three resident prophets and teachers that Barnabus and Saul are now to be sent out to *the work to which I have called them"* (Ac 13:2). This setting reveals that there were more than one gift in the church at Antioch and also that they sent out two together not one alone.

Much of the mindset today is if a person with an anointing on their life comes in to a local church he/she is just there for a time until that person starts their own work. Not all gifts are called to be head leaders of a church. Some are called to lead a portion of a church under a set leader. When these gifts fellowship with a local church prayer is necessary to find if that gift is to stay with the present ministry or sent out after further equipping, or, adding something to the local assembly.

Prayer: *Father, it has always been Your mind to have more than one gift in the local assembly. Bring whatever gifts are needed to my local church*

The Weekly Word - Week 13
Walking Out The Vision

In the "Revelation of Jesus Christ", which was spoken to John, the Lord Jesus makes Himself known as *"he who is holy, He who is true, He who has the key of David, He who opens and no one shuts, and shuts and no one opens"* (Rev 3:7). In each of the letters to the seven churches Jesus reveals Himself in a different way. Each revelation deals with a particular characteristic that the church spoken to is lacking. Jesus tells the church at Philadelphia that He is Holy and true. By stating these words He presents Himself as being one who has no imperfection, no weakness, and no untruth in Him. Then He says He is the "key of David". The Key of David speaks of kingly worship as David went after God's heart. Unlike Saul, David was a man after God's own heart and He pursued His heart thru worship. Because David sought the heart of God, He gave David an understanding of what he was supposed to do in the spreading of the kingdom. The LORD gave David a vision of his life's assignment.

The Lord has always commanded His people to follow Him, obey His word, and not compromise. At the church in Philadelphia there were those who said they were Jews, that they were circumcised, but they were not. They were not part of the body of Christ but tried to persuade the church to accept their false teachings but the church kept the word of God and did not deny His name (*authority, character*). In response, Jesus would cause these liars to worship at their feet. Worship is one of the important components in this letter to Philadelphia.

A second important component is perseverance. The Lord Jesus says *"Because you have kept My command to persevere"* He would give them the reward. We must persevere in order to obtain the promises and complete the vision that Jesus has given each of us for our lives. The devil will do anything to keep us from obtaining our inheritance and finishing our course including moving thru other men to discourage us and put obstacles in our path. But Jesus will also use difficult times to catapult us to the next level or stage of maturity and ministry. It is during the darkest times that man cries out fervently for God until the Light shines in a bleak place.

We are told to "*Write the vision and make it plain on tablets, that He may run who reads it. For the vision is yet for an appointed time, but at the end it will speak (fan as a breeze), and it will not lie. Though it tarries, wait for it, because it will surely come, it will not tarry*" (Hab. 2:2-3). Writing the vision is not a one-time deal. As the servant of God walks out the vision he has been given a new vision will begin to come into focus. Life changes and a vision will grow and expand until the person who receives the vision cannot complete it alone. It may even take generations to complete as was the vision given to Abraham. We are told that at the end the vision will speak - a breeze will come. The Holy Spirit will breathe on the vision and that which we have received will come to fruition no matter how long it takes. Remember, the Lord is the origin of the vision, not us, and He will bring it into being.

Habakkuk 2:5 finishes the thought "*Behold the proud, His soul is not upright in him; but the just shall live by his faith.*" Faith needs a direction; it needs to be applied to something. In this case it must go toward the vision that the LORD has given us. Without faith it is impossible to please God or to receive that which has been promised to us. As we progress more and more in walking out the vision given us we continue to build and expand the Kingdom of God.

Prayer: *Lord, help me to persevere in walking out the vision that you have given me of how I am to serve You. If I do not see the vision then I ask that You make it more clearly to me that I may begin to walk out the vision.*

The Weekly Word - Week 14
The Importance of the Church Being One

As we revisit the Lord's prayer in John 17, I am constantly reminded by the Lord of these words, *"I do not ask on behalf of these alone, but for those also who believe in Me through their word that they may all be one; even as Thou Father art in Me, and I in Thee, that they also may be in Us; that the world may believe that Thou didst send Me"* (v. 20 21). Much of the world does not believe that God, the Father, sent His Son, the Lord Jesus Christ to the world to deliver mankind from impending spiritual death, exclusion from the presence and glory of God. Almost 2000 years after the ascension of the Lord Jesus to the throne of God most people still do not believe. The question "Why?" must be asked, confronted, and answered not only verbally but in action. What is it about the Church that keeps people from believing that God, the Father, sent His Son to rescue mankind?

In the above verse the Lord Jesus prays that the Church would be one so that *"the world may believe that Thou didst send Me."* According to Jesus the way that the world will know that the Father sent Him is by the people of God being one. That is why the devil, our adversary, the accuser of the brethren works so hard to divide and split the Church into small companies teaching different things. Jesus continues this thought with these words, *"And the glory that thou hast given Me I have given to them; that they may be one, just as we are one. I in them, and Thou in Me, that they may be perfected in unity, that the world may know that Thou didst send Me, and didst love them, even as Thou didst love Me"* (V.22-23). It is in the people of God being one with God and the Lord Jesus that the people of the world will see that God sent the Lord Jesus.

When Jesus spoke His all-encompassing vision and mission to the disciples He commanded them, *"Go into all the world and preach the gospel to all creation. He who has believed and has been baptized shall be saved; but he who has disbelieved shall be condemned. And these signs will accompany those who have believed ;...."*(Mk 16:15-17).

Four aspects of being one with the Lord Jesus are referenced in this passage. One, preach the gospel. Two, baptize the believer. Three, demonstrate the Kingdom of God with signs and wonders. Four, do the previous three out in the world not merely within the confines of the church walls. Most of the Church presents baptism as a secondary experience. But the Lord Jesus sees it as essential. Most of the Church does not even believe that signs and wonders are for today because they are of the mindset that seeing is believing whereas the heavenly mindset says that believing is seeing. So, rather than staying within the comfort of the local church where if someone is not healed it can be overlooked, the gifts and anointings of God are to be displayed out in the world, in hospitals, nursing homes, at traffic accidents, and on the sidewalk just to name a few. Being one with God the Father and the Lord Jesus Christ is essential for the Church to be a strong witness that God sent Jesus to reconcile the world to Himself.

Prayer: *Father, I realize that it is important for the Church to be one as You and Your Son are one to show that You sent Jesus into the world to reconcile the world and destroy the power of sin. Work within my heart, O God, to walk in unity with my brothers and sisters in the truth of Your word, I pray.*

The Weekly Word - Week 15
Being With Jesus

The Lord Jesus Christ praised the church that was at Ephesus because they *"have tested those that say they are apostles and are not, and have found them liars"* (Rev. 2:2). How does the church test to find if someone is truly an apostle? The answer is found embedded in the character of those who the Lord Jesus chose to be His first apostles. We will start with Andrew since he was one of the first two to be called to be a disciple. The other one is nameless though they were both disciples of John the Baptist.

The first meeting between Jesus and Andrew occurred as Jesus appeared coming out of the wilderness after His confrontation with the devil and John announces Him as being the Lamb of God (Jn.1:35). This meeting is only recorded in the gospel according to John but it is important. When Andrew and the other disciple of John the Baptist hear and see who He is they begin to follow Him and Jesus says, *"What do you seek?"* They answered with a question, *"Rabbi, where are you staying?"* (v.37) They stayed with Him that night. Andrew and his brother Simon (Peter) lived in a town called Bethsaida on the north side of the Sea of Galilee. John was baptizing near Bethabara (Jn 1:28) which is just north of the Dead Sea about 55 miles south. Andrew and Peter were fishermen who made their livelihood on the Sea of Galilee where Jesus meets Andrew and Peter for the second time, about a year later.

On the first occasion of their meeting Andrew and the unknown disciple follow Jesus and stay with Him for the night. John the Baptist had caused so much of a stir in Israel that Andrew and Simon had travelled some 55 miles to see what was happening. When Andrew knew He had found the Messiah he followed Him, spent the night, and then the next day ran to tell his brother who subsequently meets Jesus. It was Andrew who introduced Peter to Jesus.

The next day Jesus wants to go to Galilee and sees Philip and says, *"Follow Me"* (1:43). Then Philip goes to Nathanael and tells him that they had found the one of whom Moses had spoken. Even with a little doubt Nathanael follows Philip and when Jesus sees him He says, *"Behold, an Israelite indeed, in whom is no deceit"* (v.47). Here we have two disciples who when they find the Messiah immediately go and tell others that are close to them. They immediately became voices for the Lord and then they became followers and disciples, or pupils, of the Lord.

All of this adhering to the Lord gave them a testimony that they had been with Jesus. *"Now when they saw the boldness of Peter and John, and perceived that they were uneducated and untrained men, they marveled. And they realized that they had been with Jesus"* (Act 4:13). People will realize when an apostle is in their midst because he/she does not only have the title but he/she walks in boldness, having been with Jesus. Since the Lord Jesus is not walking the earth in the flesh today we must spend time with Jesus in prayer. The night before Jesus appointed the twelve to be His apostles He spent all night in prayer with His Father. When He was finished He had the answer that He needed as to who He was to name as apostles.

The first attribute that we can see in one who is an apostle is that that person has been with the Lord. When a person spends time with Christ Jesus, He determines that He can trust that person with His anointing.

The Weekly Word - Week 16
Apostolic Characteristics

Before the discussion on the characteristics of an apostle continues it must be understood that all of the character traits espoused by the apostles and prophets of the Church are also to be displayed in the lives of the other ministry gifts to the Church as well. It is not merely the teachings that are important; it is the character of the person walking as an apostle or a prophet. The apostle Paul wrote these words to the Corinthian church concerning their division toward apostles, *"What then is Apollos? And what is Paul? Servants through whom you believed, even as the Lord gave to every man. I planted, Apollos watered, but God was causing the growth. Now he who plants and he who waters are one; but each will receive his own reward according to his own labor. For we are God's fellow workers, you are God's field, God's building"* (1 Cor. 3:5-9). In this passage Paul says that the apostle Apollos and himself are fellow workers with God, while the saints are God's field, God's building. It is this field, this building, on which the apostles and prophets labor to bring it to one glorious man in Christ.

Many people who read these messages may be apostles and prophets and I have had the privilege of "rubbing shoulders" with many in my travels and growth in the Lord. As apostles and prophets these men and women have been strong, stable, honest, loving to the house of God, and courageous. So as God continues to share with us through these writings the traits of an apostle let us consider that it is not just the teaching that is received but the character that is revealed.

The apostle John describes this event in the gospel attributed to him Jn 11:14-16, *"Then Jesus therefore said to them plainly, 'Lazarus is dead, and I am glad for your sakes that I was not there, so that you may believe; but let us go to him.' Thomas therefore, who is called Didymus, said to his fellow disciples, 'Let us also go, that we may die with him.'"* During the earlier conversation between Jesus and Martha Jesus had told Martha that Lazarus was asleep, speaking of his death. Hearing this, the apostles thought that Lazarus was asleep (v 13). So we can conclude that Thomas was not speaking of the death of Lazarus but the death of Jesus. At this point, Thomas was ready and willing to die with the Savior. He was not so ready to die when the death of the Savior occurred. But here we find Thomas bold and ready to become a martyr for the Lord, he was ready to lay down his life physically as he had already done publicly.

Before Thomas met Jesus he was a fisherman, *"There were together Simon Peter, and Thomas called Didymus, and Nathanael of Cana in Galilee, and the sons of Zebedee, and two others of His disciples"* (Jn 21:2). After Jesus was crucified they returned to their trade of fishing. Once again the Lord had to find them doing their natural vocations in order to show them that when they did His labor they would be prosperous because He would be with them.

Therefore, as fellow laborers with Christ we can go boldly forth, even into the lion's den, because we know the Savior is with us. Thomas, though he lacked understanding (Jn 20:27), was included in the eleven apostles that Jesus chose to broadcast His character as well as His Word.

Prayer: *Lord God, bring me to more of an understanding of how important it is to not only speak the truth but to live it. I know that I am an epistle of Christ, read of all men. That I glorify You in my life is most important.*

The Weekly Word - Week 17
The Tale of Two Brothers

It behooves us to once again view the apostleships of Andrew and his brother, Peter. As we have seen, Andrew became the first disciple of the Lord and he immediately ran to spread the good news to his brother Simon, called Peter.

The personalities of these two brothers are strikingly different. On the one hand, Andrew is quiet, reserved, and stays in the shadow while Simon is brazen, outgoing, boastful, and seems to want to be in the forefront and well thought of by others. In this context, every verse except one that mentions both apostles puts Peter first and Andrew second, sometimes Andrew is even mentioned after James and John the sons of Zebedee. The only description we find concerning Andrew is that he is "*Simon Peter's brother*" (Jn 1:40). We see then that Andrew is relegated to a second position to that of his brother even though he met the Lord first. The only time that Andrew is accorded a position ahead of Peter is when John describes where they are from, "*Now Philip was from Bethsaida, of the city of Andrew and Peter.*" (Jn 1:44) This description probably announces that Andrew was the older of the two which explains why he was more stable than his brother Simon. The only time that Andrew is mentioned outside of the gospels is in Acts 1:13 when the disciples return to the upper room to await the Lord. He disappears from sight after the first chapter of Acts.

Even now as Andrew leaves the horizon we can see the mark that he made upon the Church. In his short time of being included in the scriptures he had introduced his brother Simon to the Lord. On the day of Pentecost when Simon preached and delivered three thousand souls from the grasp of the devil Andrew instantly became a spiritual grandfather to three thousand people. It was not the quantity of what Andrew did but the quality of what he did by simply doing what God had inspired him to do.

Not everyone is called to go out and start a new church even though the community may need a good, on fire church. Many are called to a secondary role working with an apostle or other leader to build the Kingdom of God. Like Andrew, much will be accomplished when men and women simply do what God has called and anointed them to do, not attempting to do what is the customary and accepted way. Andrew leaves us with a picture of one that did not feel as if he needed to do a lot for the Lord as long as what he did was with the Lord.

In Matthew 25:14 - 30 we have the parable of two faithful stewards and one unfaithful steward. The steward who received ten talents and the steward who received five talents recognized the importance, the worthiness of using those talents. The steward who received one talent did not see the worth of the talent. Whether God gives us much or little to do for His Kingdom it is worth more than we will know. *"Now to Him who is able to do exceeding abundantly beyond what we ask or think, according to the power that works within us, to Him be the glory in the church and in Christ Jesus to all generations forever and ever. Amen"* (Eph 3:20-21).

If we are given what seems to be little in our eyes to do for the Kingdom we could miss out on a great reward. Consider the person who brought Billy Graham, Oral Roberts, Pat Robertson, John G. Lake, John Wesley, Bill Hamon or any number of others to know Jesus what their reward would be. Though it may have seemed trivial in the scope of all of the realm of heaven to those people who were only doing what God appointed them to do huge dividends have been paid to them because of their faithfulness.

Whether we are given much or a little to do in the Kingdom we must do it cheerfully and without reservation looking for the day of reward when we hear the words, "Well done, good and faithful servant."

Prayer: *Lord, I just want to hear the words, "Well done, good and faithful servant" when I finish my pilgrimage here on earth. I only want to accomplish what You have purposed for me to accomplish according to Your grand scheme. Order my footsteps so that I finish the work You have caused me to do and not waste time trying to do what others are called to do.*

The Weekly Word - Week 18
God's Desire For Worship

One of the major questions that needs to be answered in every believers life is "What does God desire from me in the form of worship?". Much of the Church has taken on the mentality of the Samaritan woman; *"Our fathers worshipped in this mountain, and you people say that in Jerusalem is the place where men ought to worship"* (Mat 4:20). Jesus replied, *"But an hour is coming and now is, when the true worshippers shall worship the Father in spirit and truth; for such people the Father seeks to be His worshippers"* (v.23). The Lord does not desire for us to only worship in a building one day a week, He desires us to worship Him at all times and in all situations. He desires us to worship Him in "spirit and truth" not just when the worship team leads a song.

The prophet Jonah said to God, *"While I was fainting away, I remembered the LORD; and my prayer came to Thee, into Thy holy temple"* (Jon. 2:7). The Hebrew word for prayer in this verse is *tef il law* which means supplication, intercession, or by implication a hymn. A hymn is a song that celebrates God. Jonah proclaimed that he "celebrates God" in a place other than the "House of God", in the midst of his trial, in the belly of a fish as he is eaten by the stomach acids of the fish. In the midst of his dire situation he testifies that he is celebrating God. Jonah goes on with this vow, *"But I will sacrifice to Thee with the voice of thanksgiving"* (v.9). To sacrifice something means to slaughter the flesh of an animal. When we, from our hearts, give the sacrifice of praise to the Lord we are sacrificing our flesh. We lay down our lives as we lift His name high. The phrase *"voice of thanksgiving"* means "to make a sound of adoration". The Hebrew word *"to daw"* means to extend the hand of adoration or to give a sacrifice or offering of praise or thanksgiving. It is the desire of our God that we each do this daily, not just when we gather during some set day of the week.

When king David built his tabernacle with 24 hour worship he was instructed to do so by dividing the Levites and the musicians, *"all who were to prophesy"* (1 Chr 25:1). The people who were to minister before the Lord were people who already worshipped God in their daily lives throughout the week. They did not have an off-on button like so many seem to have today; one second not paying any attention to God, the next second expecting to be in His glory.

The prophet Jeremiah speaks of this voice when he writes concerning the restoration of Judah, *"the voice of joy and the voice of gladness, the voice of the bridegroom, and the voice of the bride, the voice of those who say, 'give thanks to the LORD of hosts for the LORD is good, for His lovingkindness is everlasting; and of those who bring a thank offering unto the house of the LORD"* (Jer 33:11). The people of God are to bring an offering of praise into the place of worship, not pick it up at the door upon entering the hall or half-way through the worship. Spiritually speaking each one of us represents the "house of the Lord", the dwelling place of God. (1 Cor. 6:19)

When the Body of Christ comes together to worship the Lord it should be a choir of worshippers who are bringing what each has been doing all week individually. Even at times when we feel like we are carrying the weight of the world on our shoulders God wants us to worship Him, as Jonah did. Paul and Silas did exactly that when they were imprisoned. They did not feel sorry for themselves or get depressed, instead they worshipped God. *"But about midnight Paul and Silas were praying and singing hymns of praise to God, and the prisoners were listening to them; and suddenly there came a great earthquake, so that the foundations of the prison house were shaken; and immediately all the doors were opened, and everyone's chains were unfastened"* (Acts 16:25-26).

When the saints of God make worship a priority in their lives on a daily basis instead of thinking that a one-hour fix will get them through the week, then the Lord will show up and loosen the chains that not only bind His people but those around them who are paying attention. Even the foundations of darkness will be shaken. God desires that praise and worship be offered to Him daily so that the saints can bring a sacrificial offering into the assembly and live a life free of bondage and chains, making a difference in their realm of influence

Prayer: *Lord God, I want to be an instrument of worship. I want to worship You no matter what situation I find myself in because I know that You are there in my time of need to deliver me from all maladies. I desire to have a song in my heart of praise at all times for You are surely worthy of my praise.*

The Weekly Word - Week 19
The Need For An Apostolic Mindset

There have been times when the main focus of a meeting will not be to uplift Jesus but to rejoice in members of an assembly who have gone to different places in the world supposedly doing missionary work, or other programs. During one such meeting six people of various ages spoke on what they had done. Some went to Bosnia to take books to students and some had gone to Tennessee to work with inner-city kids in Nashville. As I listened to these six people I became perplexed concerning the absence of them sharing the "word of God" and the zero testimonies of bringing people to Christ. Not one person spoke of bringing any person to know the Lord.

The Lord reminded me in an instant of the paradigm change He is bringing to the Body of Christ as it concerns "going to all of the world." First, let me say that when I was on my first "missionary" journey to Chiapas, Mexico years ago I was very disturbed because we were not allowed to preach openly. Only during certain set times were we allowed to share the gospel and pray for people, and then, only if we were asked, lest we might offend somebody. This seems to be contrary to scripture. The Lord is about to replace the "missionary mindset" with an "apostolic mindset" where the main focus will be on the salvation of people and the planting of local churches and the raising of local elders. Instead of going out for two weeks at a time, apostolic teams will be going for months at a time, planting churches, and raising up local leaders. Along with this new mindset will come new products to perform the message. A new power of signs, wonders, gifts of healings, and working of miracles will be activated to a greater power than was seen during the restoration of the gifts during the Pentecostal and Charismatic movements in the Church.

The willingness to leave all behind and being prepared to suffer mental, physical, and emotional abuse for the cause of the Lord Jesus Christ must return to the Church. Many people have had a heart for other people groups throughout the world but many have been sent unprepared. The Church views the last words of Jesus written by Matthew as if He were talking to every saint. When Jesus said, *"Go therefore and make disciples of all nations..."* (Mat. 28:19), He was speaking to His eleven disciples who He had spent day and night with for over two years. They knew His heart, they knew His word, they knew His will, and they knew His ways. They were sent with a purpose; not to build buildings, not to raise money, not to plant gardens, not to teach schools, but to carry the truth throughout the world and plant local communities of believers, raising up local people to be leaders in those local assemblies. And they suffered persecution for it.

Only some people are to go to other nations after being anointed and prepared by the Holy Spirit; others are to stay at home where they will be more effective building the local House of God. The obligation of the leaders will be to divide those who are called and anointed to go from those who simply want to go and think it is a good idea to go. In this way the Body of Christ will be more effective in its outreach to the world.

Every saint must see his/her individual service to the Body of Christ as one that is constantly unraveling until they finish their course. Every saint's contribution to the building of the house is unique. Many do not finish their course because they are stuck in the past, following old models and old ways. Those who stand on Mount Zion with the Lamb are those who *"follow the Lamb wherever He goes"* (Rev 14:4). We must always keep our eyes on the prize and not quit, ever persevering to serve the Master with all we have; following Him wherever He goes.

Prayer: *Father, I only want to do what You have purposed for me to do. I only want to go where I am shown by You that I should go. I want to be effective in the building of Your Kingdom. Open my eyes that I might see what I am anointed to do for the Kingdom of Christ.*

The Weekly Word - Week 20
John, the Son of Zebedee

Of the twelve original apostles the one we know the most about, other than perhaps Peter, is John. John was the second son of Zebedee, the younger brother of James. He and his older brother, James, were called the "sons of thunder". Along with his brother James he asked to enjoy a privileged place in the Kingdom of Jesus Christ. *"Then James and John, the sons of Zebedee, came to Him, saying, 'Teacher, we want to do for us whatever we ask.' And He said to them, 'What do you want Me to do for you?' They said to Him, 'Grant us that we may sit, one on Your right hand and the other on Your left, in Your glory.' But Jesus said to them, 'You do not know what you ask. Are you able to drink from the cup that I drink, and be baptized with the baptism that I am baptized with?' They said to Him, 'We are able.' So Jesus said to them, 'You will indeed drink the cup that I drink, and with the baptism that I am baptized with you will be baptized; but to sit on My right hand and on My left is not mine to give, but it is for those for whom it is prepared'"* (Mk. 10:35-40). Not all requests that are made to Jesus can He fulfill because the answer is not for Him to do.

John was the youngest of the original twelve and he showed throughout the gospel attributed to his name that He was much loved by the Lord. John writes about himself more than any other author of a gospel. In fact, he dedicates three of the last four verses of his gospel to himself.

Twice in his gospel he boasts that he is the *"disciple that Jesus loved"* (Jn. 20:2; Jn. 21:7). John had such zeal, such love for the Lord, that he wanted all to know what was necessary to become "loved" of the Lord. John had a true understanding, a true revelation, of the love of God. No other gospel writer pens at length as does John concerning the love God has for those who <u>love</u> and <u>obey</u> Him. In retrospect, John's boasting about how he was loved by Jesus Christ is a testimony to all as to how to enter that fraternity. *"Whoever has My commands and obeys them, he is the one who loves Me. He who loves Me will be loved by My Father, and I too will love Him and show Myself to him"* (John 14:21). There is a special place in the heart of God for those who love and obey Him. Jesus continues, *"If anyone loves Me, he will obey My teaching. My Father will love him, and we will come to him and make our home with him. He who does not love me will not obey My teaching"* (John 14:23). The reason that John could say that Jesus loved him was because John obeyed the teachings of our Lord and loved Him.

Jesus expresses the reason for why the Father loves him in John 10:17, *"The reason My father loves Me is that I lay down My life - only to take it up again."* God loved Jesus because Jesus obeyed the Father. We see in the Garden of Eden the exact opposite. Adam and Eve did not love God and they showed that by disobeying His one restraint. Lucifer did not love God because he did that which was contrary to the word and will of God. But we see in Jesus a man who loved the Father and expressed it through obedience. Much emphasis in today's teachings is put on how God loves us but very little on how we need to love God. But it is essential that we love God to receive His love for us.

This is what we find in the relationship between the Father God and the Lord Jesus Christ. When Jesus obeyed God by giving Himself for mankind this is the testimony that God speaks, *"You are My Son; today I have become your Father"* (Heb 5:4). Love has a drawing affect. Because God loved us first we love Him. Because we love Him He loves us even more. When we show people we love them they will be attracted to us by the love of God that is within us.

Jesus relates a story of a creditor who had two debtors. These two debtors found themselves with nothing to pay but the creditor forgave both of them their debt. He ended the parable with this truth; the one who owed him the most will love him the most. Let us love the Father and all of mankind as Jesus loved the Father and obeyed Him even unto death. Love is an attribute, a fruit of the Spirit, which we cannot ignore in our walk with the Lord.

Prayer: *Father, bring me to a place where I love You so much that it can be seen by those around me so they will be drawn by Your love that is within me.*

The Weekly Word - Week 21
Prophetic Visions

1 Samuel 3:1 describes the spiritual condition of Israel at the time that Samuel was a boy, *"Now the boy Samuel ministered to the LORD before Eli. And the word of the LORD was rare in those days, visions were infrequent."* The two forms of prophecy, the spoken word and visions, are both mentioned in this verse. They were both rare and infrequent. The LORD makes a point of this because that is not the way He wants it to be in His Church. He desires His prophetic voice to be prevalent in His Church. In Proverbs 29:17-19 we read, *"Correct your son and he will give you comfort; he will also delight your soul. Where there is no vision (prophetic revelation) the people are unrestrained. But happy is he who keeps the law. A slave will not be instructed by words alone; for though he understands there will be no response."* Other words that can be substituted in verse 18 for unrestrained are "perish, uncovered, to make naked, to expose". As one seeks understanding of the prophetic vision given to him by the Holy Spirit, God will begin to mold him/her into the person that will be able to fulfill that vision.

In these three verses we see that merely being instructed will not always bring about the desired result. Often, when teaching someone a new task they must be told how to do it, and then shown how to do it, and then helped to do it by the teacher coming alongside the one learning the new task. It is not only important to have a person receive the words in his mind what needs to be accomplished, but he must grasp hold of a revelation in his heart. If the Church, or, church locally, is not given a vision, or if an individual does not receive a vision for his life, the church or the person is apt to become spiritually naked and have nothing to offer those who desire to grow in the LORD.

To illustrate this concept we can view the life of the Pharisee Saul. The Pharisee Saul knew the law by studying the word of God and when the new sect of the followers of Christ arose he went forth to slaughter them. On his way to Damascus God intervened and put Saul in darkness. At this time God was informing Saul that the pathway that he was on was only leading him into darkness. At the same time the Lord was preparing a "way" for Saul. In Damascus was a man named Ananias who received a "vision" from God concerning Saul. Ananias then went to the house where Saul was staying, laid his hands on Saul and his sight was restored.

The saints of God cannot operate on just knowing the word of God. They must also receive sight from God; a supernatural vision of what God wants each one to do in restoring the Body of Christ. This is primarily done by hearing the voice of God or through the role of the prophet. After Saul regained his sight he began to preach Jesus to the Jews; but many believers were still afraid of him. *"But Barnabas took hold of him and brought him to the apostles and described to them how he had seen the Lord on the road, and that he had talked to him, and how at Damascus he had spoken out boldly in the name of Jesus"* (Acts 9:27). Barnabas, whose name means son of prophecy, or son of consolation, came alongside Saul and defended him to the apostles. In God's grand scheme of things Ananias was sent to Saul to restore his sight and now a second prophet/apostle was beginning to engineer his acceptance into the Body of Christ.

Visions were very important in the salvation of Saul. Saul saw Ananias in a vision (Acts 9:12), Ananias saw Saul in a vision, Barnabas defends Saul and before all of this comes to pass Jesus says to Saul, *"arise, and enter the city, and it shall be told you what you must do"* (Acts 9:6). The new life of Paul the apostle was birthed from the seed sown in prophetic visions from God. This prophetic stream to the church brings life into the church and launches each person forth into his/her destiny in Christ.

Prayer: *I want to see the destiny You have for me as a cola-borer with You on this earth. Give me visions and dreams, and give other people visions and dreams that I might see what You have in store for me.*

The Weekly Word - Week 22
Servant or Son

"O, LORD, surely I am Thy servant, I am Thy servant, the son of Thy handmaid, Thou hast loosed my bonds. To Thee I will offer a sacrifice of thanksgiving, and call upon the name of the LORD" (Ps. 116:16-17). Sadly, the mindset of simply being a servant strangles many a child of God today. Many saints see themselves as a servant rather than a son or daughter of the Most High God. Although they may, but most times not, offer a sacrifice of thanksgiving to the Lord, many saints of God are still in some way in bondage to the servant mindset.

In medieval Europe there were a great many serfs who were tenant farmers who cultivated a certain plot of land that was owned by a lord. They grew their own crops and made their own clothes but worked for the lord and were bound to him. Many saints still have the mindset of being serfs to the Lord and are just happy to receive the most meager of a life. However, the free mindset acknowledges the truth that we are sons and daughters and not slaves or serfs. *"Now I say, as long as the heir is a child, he does not differ at all from a slave although he is owner of everything, but he is under guardians and managers until the date set by the father. So also we, while we were children, were held in bondage under the elemental things of the world. But when the fullness of the time came, God sent forth His Son, born of a woman, born under the law, in order that He might redeem those who were under the law, that we might receive the adoption of sons. And because you are <u>sons,</u> God has sent the Spirit of His Son into our hearts, crying, 'Abba! Father!' Therefore you are no longer a slave, but a son; and if a son, then an heir through God"* (Gal. 4:3-7). Before we became children of the Most High we were under the rule of the laws of nature but now we are free to do His will because of Jesus

Christ. There is much more joy in being a son or daughter than that of being a serf - much more freedom.

We might remember that *"Abraham had two sons, one by the bond woman and one by the free woman. But the son of the bondwoman was born according to the flesh, and the son of the free woman through the promise. And you brethren, like Isaac, are children of promise"* (Gal 4:22-23, 28). Although we are all children of promise many saints still have the mindset of being born of the bondwoman because of the natural world which wrestles against our souls and because of the lies of the devil. This mindset restricts many saints from entering into a true love relationship with the Father and coming to a true understanding of who Jesus is; not what He was, but who He is. He lived on earth and died, was resurrected and now lives in our hearts by the Spirit. He sits at the right hand of the Father in a position of power and authority as He reigns over the entire universe.

If the saints of God can be unshackled from the mindset of living as a serf and begin living as an heir to all things a freedom will come that will unshackle the Church from the mindset of a serf to the glory to which she is called. *"For it was fitting for Him, for whom are all things, and through whom are all things, in bringing many sons to glory, to perfect the author of their salvation through sufferings"* (Heb. 2:10). God has decided to bring many sons into glory, starting with the Lord Jesus Christ. *"For I consider the sufferings of this present time are not worthy to be compared with the glory that is to be revealed in us"* (Rom. 8:18). Many saints are waiting desperately for God to reveal His glory to them when He wants to reveal His glory through them.

The serf mentality must be eliminated from the Body of Christ so that the Bride of Christ can come forth in all of her splendor and show the glory of God to the world.

Prayer: *Father, change my mindset from a serf servant mentality to knowing who I am in Christ. I am a child of God; a son or a daughter of the King. May I realize that through the guidance of the Holy Spirit?*

The Weekly Word - Week 23
Compassion

If we desire to be like our Father in heaven we must begin to see Him as He is. The Lord Jesus said, *"Truly, truly I say unto you, the Son can do nothing of Himself, unless it is something He sees the Father doing; for whatever the Father does, these things the Son also does in like manner"* (Lk. 5:19). How did Jesus see His Father, and what did He see His Father doing? One component of His Father that Jesus saw was compassion. Five times the Psalmist recognizes God as being compassionate. *"But He, being compassionate, forgave their iniquity, and did not destroy them ;"* (Ps. 78:38). *"But You, O God, are a God full of compassion and gracious, longsuffering and abundant in mercy and truth"* (Ps. 86:15). *"He has made His wonderful works to be remembered; the LORD is gracious and full of compassion"* (Ps 111:4). When it was necessary Jesus was moved as His Father was moved - with compassion.

We also are told to move in compassion as our Father in heaven is moved. The Lord Jesus said this about the Father, *"for He Himself is kind to ungrateful and evil men"* (Lk 6:35). Then He tells us in the very next verse, *"Be merciful, just as your Father is merciful."* We are to be no more merciful and no less merciful than our heavenly Father. Many times man tries to be more merciful than God and it just turns out to be from a seed of pride or guilt.

Most of the time the Hebrew word translated as compassion actually means "pity, to feel sympathy, for the bowels (inward affection) to yearn". The Lord showed this compassion for the unsaved multitude (Mat. 9:36), by healing of the sick (Mt. 14:14), in feeding the 4000 (Mat. 15:32), by restoring sight to the two blind men who asked to receive their sight (Mat. 20:29-34), in the leper who asked to become clean (Mk. 1:41), in the

Gadarene demoniac who came and worshipped Him and was delivered of an unclean spirit (Jn 5:1-8,19), in the mute boy out of whom Jesus cast a mute spirit after his father confessed that he believed that Jesus could perform the miracle ((Mk. 9:22), and in the woman's only son whom Jesus raised from the dead, showing compassion (Lu 7:13-14).

It has been said that it took John Wimber 100 attempts to heal a person before he saw one healed. The question comes to mind as to whether it took him that long to unlock the compassion that the Lord had put in his inward part so that healing would come forth. Yes, it is true that healing can come by faith or by the use of the "gifts of healing" which is given to members of the Body of Christ by the Holy Spirit. But the Church has seen such a sporadic demonstration of the signs of healing, deliverance, miracles, and salvation of the multitude that we must begin to desire the work of compassion that can bring about these results more often than what we have seen to this date.

As we go about attempting to do, or doing, the things that we see our Father do we must also go about being as He is in this world. We must move out of a heart of compassion, pity or sympathy, and not merely because we believe. We must do what we see the Father doing; acting out of compassion instead of mere faith, Lord, help our unbelief, or because the word says so. God moved with compassion because that is who He is. The Lord Jesus moved with compassion because that is what He saw the Father do. We must be moved with compassion to follow the example of what our Lord showed us to do and what to be.

Prayer: *"Lord, unlock the compassion that you have put within each one of us that we might be more of an impact for you in this world."*

The Weekly Word - Week 24
Hidden In The Day of Anger

Zephaniah 2:1-3 says, "*Gather yourselves together, yes, gather together, O undesirable nation, before the decree is issued, or the day passes like chaff, before the LORD's anger comes upon you! Seek the LORD, all the meek of the earth, who have upheld His justice. Seek righteousness, seek humility. It may be that you will be hidden in the day of the LORD's anger.*"

The LORD gives a command in this verse for the people of Judah and Jerusalem (1:4) to assemble themselves unto Him; to seek the LORD and His righteousness (Mat. 6:33). He tells Judah to do this "*before the LORD's anger comes upon you*" warning them of what is to come. In 2:1 He speaks of Judah being a nation that is not desired. Even the LORD is not longing for Judah because Judah has walked in idolatry, "*I will stretch out My hand against Judah, and against all the inhabitants of Jerusalem. I will cut off every trace of Baal from this place, the names of the idolatrous priests with the pagan priests - those who worship the host of heaven on the housetops; those who worship and swear oaths by the LORD, but who also swear by Milcom*" (Zep. 1:4-5).

The entire writing of Zephaniah is a warning of punishment coming from the LORD because of disobedience. There is punishment for "*those who have turned back from following the LORD, and have not sought the LORD, nor inquired of Him*" (Zeph. 1:6). Another way of stating this verse is "those who have become apostatized or backslidden, and have not strived after the LORD in worship or prayer, nor pursued after Him." But within this writing of devastation there is hope for those who seek the LORD.

We are in the age of the Laodicean church where it is commonplace for the saints of God to sit back, trusting in the initial experience of receiving the work done on the cross but progressing no further. Much of the Church has become satisfied with the beginning stage of knowing Him and has not pursued Him intimately. But Paul told us that it was his desire to *"be found in Him, not having my own righteousness, which is from the law, but that which is through faith in Christ, the righteousness which is from God by faith; that I may know Him and the power of His resurrection, and the fellowship of His sufferings, being conformed to His death, if, by any means, I may attain to the resurrection from the dead"* (Phil 3:9-11). This desire of Paul takes us beyond the cross. It takes us beyond the grave to a new position in Him. It is a position of power and authority.

But instead, as the people of Judah, many in the Church have the belief that all that is required of them is to come to church on Sunday and look good for the minister, because "he does not know what kind of life I live during the week." A superficial salvation has overcome the children of God. Instead of being overcomers many are overcome by the world yet sit in the pew or a chair every Sunday putting on a happy face. We are told to seek the LORD, His righteousness, and humility *"that you may be hidden in the day of the LORD's anger."* The day of the LORD's anger is coming and everyone needs to take the necessary steps so as to be hidden on that day.

The first step is to assemble together as the children of Israel were assembled. When they walked through the desert they were not scattered all over the countryside, they were together, in four ranks. When they camped, the tribes camped as one, not in small little groups separate from one another. On the day of Pentecost the disciples were together in one place where the Holy Spirit was initially poured out. Is there any record that any person not in the upper room received the initial outpouring of the Holy Spirit? No! He was only poured out on those who were assembled in the upper room. The first step toward preparing for the indignation that God is going to pour out on the earth is to "gather together". This may call for some churches to unite, having multidimensional ministries under one roof.

Or, it may call for some churches to stop existing all together by coming under another's leadership. As the Body of Christ comes together God can then bring judgment upon our enemies as He has promised.

God promises to destroy Gaza, Ashkelon, Ashdod, and Ekron; all cities of the Philistines which at the present is the Palestinian hold out with Hemas in leadership against Israel. He has promised to judge Moab and Ammon who have taken much of the territory on the eastside of Jordan from Israel which is present day Syria and Jordan. But God will spare His righteous who take refuge in the name of the LORD (Zep. 3:12).

Prayer: *Lord, help Your body to become one, putting away the strife, competition, and jealousy that we see today among different churches. By Your guiding hand, bring us together as one that we might show the world the power of Your resurrection.*

The Weekly Word - Week 25
Selfishness

The Body of Christ, the family of God, lives in a selfish, corrupt, "me first" world. As the world would have it, everything is "Me first." Many citizens of the world have a mindset that looks to the government for the provision they need. Medicaid, medicare, social security, unemployment benefits, and food stamps are just a few of the ways people think "Me first". This author once on unemployment for a year and thought nothing of what harm was being done to the economy through selfishness. I had worked hard (less than 6 years) for the right to receive money that could have been used in a more beneficial way.

Sad to say this "Me first" attitude is found in many believers, leaders and pew sitters, in the Body of Christ today. Paul, the apostle, wrote to the Philippians *"Let nothing be done through selfish ambition or conceit, but in lowliness of mind let each esteem others better than himself. Let each of you look out not only for his own interests, but also for the interests of others"* (Phil.2:3-4). The Lord Jesus tells us that *"he who is greatest among you, let him be as the younger, and he who governs as he who serves"* (Lk. 22:26). The Greek word translated as "serve" in this passage has three basic meanings - to be an attendant, or wait upon as a host, friend, or teacher. Technically it means "to act as a Christian deacon".

Each one of us is to think of our brothers and sisters as superior to ourselves. In this vein of thinking we must consider that it is more important for our brother or sister to succeed in his callings and anointings than ourselves. The teacher must think it is more important for his hearers to succeed and they, in turn, must consider it more important for their teacher to succeed. The Apostle and Prophet must consider it more important for his/her disciples to be empowered from on high with the manifest presence of the Lord and each disciple must consider it more important for the Apostle or Prophet by whom they are being equipped to succeed. Each husband is to consider it more important for his wife to succeed and each wife is to consider it more important for her husband to succeed in the callings of God.

The children of God have also been called to serve the world. Not so much in worldly ways as in spiritual ways. It has been said that hungry people won't listen to the preaching of Jesus Christ unless they are fed first. Jesus did not feed the five thousand because He wanted them to hear the gospel. The multitudes had been following Him and listening to the gospel without any concern for eating for days. The Body of Christ needs to walk in a spiritual level so that the world begins to be drawn unto righteousness. *"Blessed are those that hunger and thirst for righteousness for they shall be filled"* (Mat. 5:6). It has been said that some people are so spiritually minded that they are no earthly good. Actually, the more spiritually minded one is the more earthly good they become. The Body of Christ is not on earth to preserve the status quo, it is here to change the world; to transform the kingdoms of this world into the *"Kingdom of our Lord and of His Christ, and He shall reign forever and ever"* (Rev. 11:15).

The Body of Christ can powerfully do this by serving. *"And whosoever desires to be first among you, let him be your slave - just as the Son of Man did not come to be served, but to serve, and to give His life a ransom for many"* (Mat. 20:27-28). The Body of Christ is called to serve one another and the world by dying to the flesh.

Prayer: *Father, give the rightful mindset to us, Your children, so that we become servants of one another and to the world. As our Lord Jesus went about serving we desire to also go about serving, bringing glory to You.*

The Weekly Word - Week 26
Jesus the Good Shepherd

In the Gospel according to John Chapter 10 Jesus gives a lengthy explanation concerning Him being the Good Shepherd explaining how He knows His sheep and is known of His. The entire monologue begins with verse 1 and continues through verse 16, with the main focus on verse 10. We find in this passage a contrast that the Lord Jesus Christ makes between Himself and the ruler of darkness. Verse one says, *"Truly, truly, I say to you, he who does not enter by the door into the fold of the sheep, but climbs up some other way, he is a thief and a robber."* There is obviously another way besides coming through the door to enter into the sheepfold. That is how the Church gets wolves and goats in the midst.

In this passage Jesus makes it clear that He is the door and the Good Shepherd of the flock. The Good Shepherd watches over His sheep and leads them to green pastures and they know His voice. One who is of the flock of God will not follow another voice - the voice of division, rebelliousness, wrath, jealousy, murder, and uncleanness. They will not follow the voice that is preaching false doctrine but will reprove those who speak a weak, destructive word. The Lord describes Himself as one who would lay down His life for the sheep instead of having the sheep lay down theirs for him.

Now, verse 10, *"The thief comes only to steal, and kill, and destroy; I have come that you might have life and might have it abundantly."* The word "abundantly" in this passage speaks of having superabundance in quantity or a superior quality of life. The thief comes to cause man to have a subpar life; a life less than what we were designed to experience in Christ. But Christ came that we might enjoy life in Him to the fullest. He came to restore the relationship that the first Adam had with the

LORD. He calls us to have dominion, to reign over all things, to be victorious. He has given us power to defeat the obstacles of this life and the works of the devil.

Many have come preaching false teachings in the name of our Lord which is why there is much division in Christendom. Jesus said, "*I am the good shepherd and I know My own, and My own know Me*" (v14). If we consider ourselves as being owned by our Lord then we realize that we are not our own to do as we please or teach things outside of the truth. By living unto Jesus we can have "life more abundantly". "*All those who came before Me are thieves and robbers, but the sheep did not hear them*" (v.8). The Lord says here that those who do not speak the truth have come to steal from and plunder the lives of those living on earth. He considers them as doing the work of our enemy. Jesus alone brought the truth of God to man because he alone was sent by God. We can except no other as our Shepherd. Only in Him is a greater quantity and superior quality of life. Many have said that they want to "live life to the fullest" but that can only be done by losing ourselves in the life of our Lord Jesus Christ.

Prayer: *Lord Jesus, we ask that You sharpen our ears to hear only Your voice, and none other. As we follow You, we ask for discernment to know when someone besides You is attempting to lead us. We ask that we enter into that life that is full of the riches of the glory of God that You came to earth, died, and was resurrected in order to make that life available to us.*

The Weekly Word - Week 27
The Full Commission of Christ

The 21ˢᵗ century Church has a shortsighted view as to what the Lord Jesus Christ was commissioned to do when He came to earth. Much of the Church only sees that the Lord came for the purpose of saving men's souls; that the preaching of the gospel is the only important work He was sent to accomplish. This is far from the full truth and the Church must once again embrace the totality of the commissioning that was upon Him. The gospel according to Luke reveals five of the nineteen, or more, reasons why the Lord was sent by the Father, *"The Spirit of the LORD is upon Me, because He anointed Me to preach the gospel to the poor. He has sent Me to proclaim release to the captives, and recovery of sight to the blind, to set free those who are downtrodden, to proclaim the favorable year of the LORD"* (Lk. 4:18-19).

Most of the Church will agree with the first and second assignments that were bestowed upon the Lord by His Father. The first task was to preach the gospel of the Kingdom to the poor in spirit. As He preached the gospel He evangelized those who heard and received His powerful words. When one evangelizes he preaches the gospel without regard to the results. The second concern the Lord came to fulfill was to release the captives, or, pardon men for sins committed. Most of the Church will agree with those two assignments.

The third mission the Lord came to initiate was to proclaim recovery of sight to the blind. The Word of God illustrates two different ways of recovering sight - spiritually and physically. In Matthew 9:27-29 we see an example of the natural restoration of sight. In this passage of scripture two blind men followed the Lord crying, *"Have mercy on us, Son of David."* After Jesus had entered a house the two men approached Him and Jesus asked, *"Do you believe that I am able to do this?"* To which they replied, "Yes." The Lord then layed His hands on their eyes and said, *"Be it done to you according to your faith."* The Word of God then testifies, *"And their eyes were opened"* (v.30). This account is definitely relating an incident where Jesus restored natural sight to men and it must not be misconstrued in an attempt to twist this account to say that He only restores spiritual sight today. The Lord is still willing and able to restore physical sight to people today.

The restoration of spiritual sight is dealt with in Matthew 15:12-14 where the disciples of our Lord were disconcerted over the fact that the Pharisees were offended by the words of Jesus. His response to this was, *"Let them alone, they are blind guides of the blind. And if a blind man guides a blind man, both will fall into a ditch."* Was the Lord saying that the Pharisees were physically blind? No! He was saying that the law and the traditions of men had blinded them from seeing the truth.

The fourth purpose that the Lord Jesus was sent to accomplish was to *"set free those who are downtrodden"* or, as it says in the 1599 Geneva Bible "to set at liberty those who are bruised". *"Then there was brought to Him a demon-possessed man who was blind and dumb, and He healed him, so that the dumb man spoke and saw"* (Mat. 12:22). The Lord not only healed the sick but He cast out demons from those who were tormented by evil spirits. In Matthew 15:21-28 He cast out a demon of the Syrophoenician woman's daughter by the word of His mouth in addition to her faith.

In the 21st century we must continue to follow His example by   preaching the full gospel including healing the sick and setting the demon-possessed free.

Prayer: *Lord Jesus, I have been limited in my faith because I have not heard all that You came to say and do in this present hour. Lord, I ask that my eyes be opened to all that You desire to accomplish in this season.*

The Weekly Word - Week 28
The Full Commission (Part 2)

Continuing with the subject of "Why did Jesus come?" we see that Jesus came to do the will of His Father. He did not come to do his own will; He came to do His Father's will. John, the apostle, writes these words of Jesus, *"I can of Myself do nothing. As I hear, I judge, and My judgment is righteous, because I do not seek My own will but the will of the Father who sent Me"* (Jn 5:30). Here the Lord Jesus expresses to the hearer that He is able to execute righteous judgment because of the way He hears what the Father is saying. In the expression of hearing what the Father is saying it is understood that it is the Father's will and not His own that Jesus desires to fulfill. If the Lord would ever come to a place where His will interfered with hearing the Father's will than He would not be able to judge righteously. The Lord tells us *"Do not judge according to appearance, but judge with righteous judgment"* (Jn 7:24). We are able to do judge righteously by seeking the will of God in all that we hear, and not seeking our own will, just as the Lord Jesus sought to do the will of the Father.

The Lord continues with this focus on His assignment with these words, *"But I said to you that you have seen Me and yet do not believe. All that the Father gives Me will come to Me and the one who comes to Me I will by no means cast out. For I have come down from heaven, not to do My own will, but the will of Him who sent Me. This is the will of the Father who sent Me, that of all He has given Me I should lose nothing, but should raise it up at the last day. And this is the will of Him who sent Me, that everyone who sees the Son and believes in Him may have everlasting life, and I will raise him up at the last day"* (Jn 6:36-40). The Lord makes it pretty clear with these words that He came to do the Father's will and not His own. As we follow

His example we must desire to do His will and not our own; to build His Kingdom and not our own; to exalt His name and not our own.

The Lord Jesus says in this passage that it is the Father's will that Jesus would lose nothing of what God has given Him. This passage is talking about men's souls. The Father does not want any person who has come to Jesus to be lost, but to be raised up at the last day. He definitely is talking about His Shepherds role in this passage. Every sheep that the Father gives to the Lord Jesus, the Shepherd of our souls, He desires to be raised up on the last day. This makes it essential that one of two things happens in every local body of believers. Either the leader must exhibit a heart of a shepherd, or, the leader of the house must team up with another who has a shepherd's heart to feed the sheep in green pastures beside still waters.

Many men and women in leadership roles in local assemblies have an anointing other than a shepherd's (pastoral) anointing. This has caused many sheep to leave the flock and become wounded or even die because they were unable to "hear" what the Father was saying. Whenever the Father speaks it is always with the intention of elevating the one spoken to from the level he is now walking to a higher level of walking with Him. It is always to deposit His will, ways, and word into the heart of man. The Lord Jesus often used the expression *"Him who has ears to hear, let Him hear."* We need to be attentive as to how we hear what the Father speaks in order to do His will.

Prayer*: Father, I submit my will to You. I only desire to do Your will but I cannot do it if I do not know what Your will is for my life. Father, I open my heart to hear what You have to say to me on a daily basis concerning Your will for my life.*

The Weekly Word - Week 29
Walking in Unbelief

Matthew 17:14 illustrates the consequences of walking in unbelief. Verse 14 speaks of a man who brings his demon possessed
son to Jesus for help. He informs the Lord that he had taken his
son to the disciples but were unable to help him. Jesus responds
"O unbelieving and perverted generation, how long shall I be
with you? Bring him here to Me." The disciples then came to
Jesus asking why they could not cast out the evil spirit and Jesus
answers, *"Because of the littleness of your faith; for truly I say*
to you, if you have faith as a mustard seed, you shall say to this
mountain, 'Move from here to there', and it shall move; and
nothing shall be impossible to you" (v 20).

In this scene Jesus is speaking to two different audiences.
First, He speaks to an unbelieving generation who must look to
others, i.e. the disciples, to perform what they should be able to
do themselves through faith in the power of God. Secondly, He
speaks to the disciples concerning their lack of faith. He tells
them that if they have the faith, i.e. the persuasion or conviction,
only as large as a grain of mustard seed that they are equipped
to do all things. The implication of what Jesus is saying concerning the mustard seed is not its size but the nature of a grain
of mustard seed. Though a grain of mustard seed is small, by
nature it has a stinging quality. To put it one way, you are going to put a hurtin' on that thing that you rebuke if you are so
persuaded.

In this era of many people being forced to walk in false humility a spirit of unbelief has come upon the Church. The Lord
Jesus tells us that if we are completely persuaded that He has
given us the power to move mountains nothing is impossible to
us. Jesus says, *"You shall say to this mountain, 'Move from here*
to there." He does not tell us to pray for Him to do it; He tells

us to do it. Jesus told the disciples to wait in Jerusalem until they received power from on high. That power is far more than speaking in tongues or prophesying. It includes the working of miracles also. We must only be persuaded that with the power of God inside of us that we are able to do it. In Mark 16:17 Jesus tells us that we shall cast out demons because He has given us the authority to do so as we walk in His name (*character and authority*). Jesus is not a liar so we must believe what He has said.

A second point pertaining to moving mountains is that a mountain must be told to go someplace other than where it exists. If it is not told to go someplace else it just remains where it is. "*What are you, O great mountain? Before Zerubbabel you will become a plain; and he will bring forth the capstone with shouts of 'Grace, grace to it'*" (Zech. 4:7). Jesus tells us, His disciples, to tell the mountain to go someplace other than where it is at the present time. We can also tell a mountain to become a plain. One can't just tell them to be removed; they also must be told where to go - the pit is a good place for them. One mountain we can all tell to go to the pit is the spirit "division" which has been displayed since the time of Martin Luther. It has run alongside the restoration work God has brought to the Church but has kept her from fulfilling her destiny which is only brought by being in unity.

Prayer: *Father, I ask for the faith that I need to believe that I have been empowered to move mountains according to the Word of God and the Holy Spirit who dwells in me and with me.*

The Weekly Word - Week 30
Praying For Leaders (Part 1)

One of the greatest concerns every saint of God should have is the continual assaults that the enemy plays against the leaders of the church. Often there is a misconception that the leaders of the church are too spiritual to fall into the traps that our enemy sets for them. The Word of God says that, *"your adversary, the devil, as a roaring lion, walks about seeking whom he can devour"* (1 Pe. 5:8). This especially means those who are in the forefront of guiding the Church to its declared destiny. Praying for spiritual leaders is the responsibility of every saint of God.

In Ephesians 4:11 the apostle Paul mentions five gifts that were given to the Church when the Lord Jesus ascended to the throne, *"And He gave some as apostles, and some as prophets, and some as evangelists, and some as pastors and teachers."* These gifts were given to the Church as a whole to equip her for the work of service and other essential purposes. The important truth to understand is that these positions of authority and service are <u>gifts</u> to the Church. These <u>gifts</u> are to be received with thanksgiving, love, and respect.

Paul also speaks of the order in which God has placed these gifts in local assemblies, *"And God has appointed in the church, first apostles, second prophets, third teachers, then miracles, then gifts of healings, helps, administrations, various kinds of tongues"* (1 Cor. 12:28). In this list Paul begins with ascension gifts given to the church by the Lord Jesus and finishes with certain gifts given to the church by the Holy Spirit. Hidden in this verse are not only the titles of those who lead the church, but the functions of those who lead the church by the anointing of God.

Now that it has been exposed as to who God tells the church to pray for the church must be informed concerning how to pray for these leaders. To begin with Paul writes to Timothy, a son in the faith, *"First of all then, I urge that entreaties and prayers, petitions and thanksgivings, be made on behalf of all men, for kings and all who are in authority, in order that we may lead a tranquil and quiet life in all godliness and dignity. This is good and acceptable in the sight of God our Savior"* (1 Tim 2:1-2). It has <u>never</u> been the desire or purpose of secular governmental leaders to set an environment of godliness. That is the responsibility of the leaders of the church. So within these instructions to Timothy Paul is explaining that the spiritual leaders of the Church are to be prayed for; that entreaties, petitions, and thanksgiving be given for those who are serving the people of God.

By praying for the leaders of the church, and the Church as a whole, much more territory will be taken back from the enemy and more victories shall be won. When Israel went to battle against Amalek we read the following, *"So it came about when Moses held his hand up, that Israel prevailed, and when he let his hand down Amalek prevailed"* (Ex. 17:11). Moses only had strength to hold his hands up for a short time and Israel prevailed when his hands were held up. But when he got weak the enemy prevailed. So it is with the spiritual leaders of each church. Their hands <u>must</u> be held up in prayer by the saints of God.

In praying for our spiritual leaders we show God that we have received them as those who *"watch over our souls, as those who will give account"* (Heb 13: 17). This allows the leaders to *"do this with joy, and not with grief, for this would be unprofitable for you."* Not listening to and not following the Word that is taught is unprofitable to the one who ignores what is being taught. On the other hand, if prayers are not being offered to God for the leaders they may not hear what God wants for them to feed the flock. Prayers for the leaders of each church are necessary for the people of God to grow. And each saint of God is responsible to pray for their leader(s).

Prayer: *Father God, I pray for my spiritual leaders that have been placed over me for my good. I ask that You lead them and guide them in how they are to equip me for the work of ministry. I pray that You protect them from the wiles of the devil as the devil fights against them in an attempt to hurt the Body of Christ.*

The Weekly Word - Week 31
The Tale of Two Men

As Jesus went about preaching the Kingdom of God many people came to Him saying, "*John performed no sign, but all the things John spoke about this man were true*" (John 10:41). John the Baptist had ministered throughout the land of Judah preaching the Kingdom of God and pointing to the one who would come after him, which was the Lord Jesus. In this verse, the word testifies that John the Baptist did no signs, no miracles. The ministry of John was restricted to preaching the Kingdom of God and calling all people to repentance.

The incident that precedes this statement describes how the Jews surrounded Jesus and demanded of Him to tell them if He were the Christ. To these demands Jesus responded, "*If I do not do the works of My Father, do not believe Me; but if I do, though you do not believe Me believe the works, that you may know and believe that the Father is in Me and I in Him*" (v. 37-38). According to the words of Jesus it was not the words that He spoke that proved who He was but the miracles He performed. John, the Baptist, did no miracles but Jesus said to believe in who He was because of the miracles He performed.

Even though John did no miracles everything He said pertaining to Jesus was true, "*all the things that John spoke about this man were true.*" After John was murdered by Herod the Lord Jesus came preaching the Kingdom and calling people to repentance, just as John had done. This was the testimony of Jesus, "*But I have a greater witness than John's; for the works the Father has given Me to finish - the very works that I do - bear witness of Me, that the Father has sent Me*" (Jn. 5:36). John bear witness to who Jesus was but the works that Jesus performed were a greater witness as to who He was.

John was sent by God to be *"The voice of one crying in the wilderness, make ready the way of the LORD. Make His paths straight"* (Mat. 3:3) fulfilling the prophecy of Isaiah 40:3. Jesus was anointed by God according to Isaiah 61:1, *"The Spirit of the LORD is upon Me; because He anointed Me to preach the gospel to the poor. He has sent Me to proclaim release to the captives, and recovery of sight to the blind, to set free those who are downtrodden, to proclaim the favorable year of the LORD"* (Lk. 4:17-18). Both received many disciples who followed them even though the majority continued to disbelieve their words and who they were.

In the time after John the Baptist was killed and the Lord was crucified there were disciples of both John and Jesus still living in the land. This is shown in Acts 19 where Paul meets some disciples of John the Baptist in Ephesus, *"Did you receive the Holy Spirit when you believed?"* he asked. *"We have not so much as heard whether there is a Holy Spirit,"* they answered. *"And he said to them, 'Into what then were you baptized?" So they said, 'Into John's baptism.' Then Paul said, 'John indeed baptized with a baptism of repentance, saying to the people that they should believe on Him who would come after him, that is, on Christ Jesus.' When they heard this, they were baptized in the name of the Lord Jesus. And when Paul had laid hands on them, the Holy Spirit came upon them, and they spoke with tongues and prophesied"* (Acts 19:2-6).

In the story recounted in Acts 19:2-6, three experiences are partaken of by the disciples of John. First, they were baptized by John into John's baptism of repentance prior to their meeting with Paul. Second, they were baptized a second time into the Lord Jesus Christ after they received the truth that Jesus was the one that was to come after John. Third, when Paul laid hands on them they received the Holy Spirit - for they had not received Him as of yet. Since the reformation of the Church has come in waves rather than all at once there has been much controversy concerning water baptism and the Baptism of the Holy Spirit. Acts chapter 19, along with other passages, clearly distinguishes between these two experiences. The disciples of John that Paul addressed wanted all that they could receive from the Lord regardless of the expense. Acts 4 declares that there was a subsequent filling of the Holy Spirit later in the lives of those who had already received Him on the Day of Pentecost. *"And when they had prayed, the place where they had gathered together was shaken, and they were all filled with the Holy Spirit and began to speak the word of God with boldness"* (Acts 4:31). This reality reveals to the people of God that we can never be satisfied with where we are.

In the Church of the 21st century there are followers of both of these two men representing two branches as it were of the same tree - Jesus. The one branch knows who Jesus is and speaks the things concerning Him that are true. The other branch knows Him, speaks the things that are true concerning Him, and performs the signs that prove that they are followers of the one true God - Jehovah, The Great I Am, the LORD God Almighty. The Holy Spirit speaks today that it is time for these two branches to become one living branch of the same Olive Tree.

The Weekly Word - Week 32
Praying For Leaders (Part 2)

The first major attribute that must be held up in prayer when praying for leaders is that they would receive "utterance" from God. There are plenty of ministers and speakers today who can lecture for an hour or more, going down all types of rabbit trails to make this point or that point and really say very little of any consequence in that hour. But that it is not what is meant by the word "utterance". In Ephesians 6:18-20 Paul gives the saints at Ephesus some instructions on prayer and a request for prayer. *"With all prayer and petition pray at all times in the Spirit, and with this in view, be on the alert with all perseverance and petition for all the saints, and pray on my behalf, that utterance may be given to me in the opening of my mouth, to make known with boldness the mystery of the gospel, for which I am an ambassador in chains; that in proclaiming it I may speak boldly, as I ought to speak."* The first request Paul makes is that he would receive utterance. The word "utterance" is a translation of the Greek word *"logos"* which is what is rendered as the written word of God, *logos*, or, Jesus Christ Himself. It simply means something said. In this reference it is the Word spoken by God. Paul is making the request for "utterance" so that he might *"make known with boldness the mystery of the gospel"*. He does not ask for prayers that he might come up with witty sayings, catch phrases, funny stories, or life examples. He simply wants to make the gospel known.

The apostle Paul believes that the prayers of the saints are necessary for the ministry given to him by God to be fruitful and anointed. He does not rely on all of the knowledge that he has come to possess over his many years of being a Pharisee, and now a teacher of righteousness, to cause him to be fruitful in the things of God. Paul did not wish to speak the weak words of man with man's wisdom; he desired to hear words from the throne. He may have been informed of the conversation that the Lord Jesus had with His Father. *"Now my soul is troubled, and what shall I say, 'Father, save me from this hour? But for this purpose I came into this hour. Father, glorify your name.' Then a voice came from heaven, saying, 'I have both glorified it and will glorify it again.' Therefore the people who stood by and heard it said that it had thundered. Others said, 'An angel has spoken to Him.' Jesus answered and said, 'This voice did not come because of Me, but for your sake'"* (Jn. 12:27-30). Whereas Jesus heard the voice of His Father clearly some heard an angel and yet others heard thunder. Some who were standing by could not discern or did not hear the voice of God.

This is the way Paul wanted to speak. He believed that it was worthless if he would speak words that did not carry the anointing and the authority of God. He wanted to speak words that came directly from the throne room of heaven. Jesus said these words, *"The words that I speak to you I do not speak on My own authority, but the Father who dwells in Me does the work"* (Jn. 14:10). If Jesus relied on the Father to give Him the words that he spoke, how much more do the ministers who speak in His name need to rely on Him to furnish the words?

Paul only wanted to speak the words that were given him by the Spirit of God because he knew, *"It is the Spirit who gives life; the flesh profits nothing, the words that I speak to you they are Spirit, and they are life"* (Jn. 6:63). In speaking of the ministry he had received Paul says, *"Not that we are adequate in ourselves to consider anything as coming from ourselves, but our adequacy is from God, who also made us adequate as servants of a new covenant, not of the letter, but of the Spirit, for the letter kills, but the Spirit gives life"* (2 Cor. 3:5-6). Anytime Paul preached he wanted the hearer to receive life and not just dead words. He knew that if it came from him, his thoughts and imagination, it would only produce death; but if it came from the Spirit, the hearer would receive life.

Prayer: *Father, I ask that You continually give (name of leader(s) utterance from the throne so that the hearers would receive life and not death.*

The Weekly Word - Week 33
Praying For Leaders (Part 3)

Before this series of messages goes any further it must be explained that no matter where one is in ministry there should be somebody who is responsible for that person's spiritual growth. If you are a saint of God with no "proclaimed" ministry but are in the process of being equipped for the work of service those would be the leaders of the House of Worship that you attend. This would include any of the five ascension gifts Jesus gave to the Church plus any other leader directly associated with you. If you are on the worship team you would be praying for the worship leader for anointing and to have the right attitude and to properly serve those on the team. If you are in ministry there would be another minister who is responsible to watch for your soul. If you are the head of a local church you would have an elder of the district, region, or one to whom you are submitted. In addition, prayers should be made for those in horizontal relationships as well as perpendicular.

One aspect that needs to be lifted up to our heavenly Father in prayer is for those who we pray for to speak the word of God with authority. If the saints of God are to grow up in the nurture and admonition of the Lord they must be taught with words that have authority. *"And so it was, when Jesus had ended these sayings, that the people were astonished in His teaching, for He taught them as one having authority, and not as the scribes"* (Mar. 7:28-29). Jesus taught with authority because He received it from His Father. He did not receive authority from other men, because of some position He had been awarded, or because of a title that He carried. His authority came from God and so His words carried that authority. This "authority" can be distinguished between a person who gives an "I think" statement and a person who gives a prophecy to another or to a congregation.

The "I think" will have no authority whereas the prophecy will have the authority of the author, God. When a person speaks with no authority no life can be given.

In Acts 19:13-16 we have the illustration of some Jewish exorcists who attempted to deliver a man from an evil spirit in the name of Jesus. These men were not believers in Jesus but presumptively attempted to cast out an evil spirit using the name of Jesus. The evil spirit answered the men, *"Jesus I know, and Paul I know, but who are you."* If the leaders of the church do not have a relationship with the Lord Jesus, and are not submitted to His words, they will have no authority to do the works of God. No relationship equals no authority.

Jesus spoke these words to explain that He was a messenger sent by the Father, *"The words that I speak to you I do not speak on My own authority; but the Father who dwells in Me does the works"* (Jn. 14:10). The Lord Jesus witnessed that His authority came from God because he was submitted to His Father. Therefore, when He spoke the words He heard the Father saying they had authority. When He spoke with this authority the hearts of men were convicted with the words that He spoke. This is the authority in which Jesus has called His servants to walk.

In 1 Corinthians 14:24-25 we read this passage *"But if all prophesy, and an unbeliever or ungifted man enters, he is convicted by all, he is called to account by all; the secrets of his heart are disclosed; and so he will fall on His face and worship God, declaring that God is certainly among you"*. As a side note, Paul writes here that if "all prophesy". He puts no limit on the number of who can prophesy. The word prophesy means "to foretell events, speak under inspiration". In this passage it could mean either definition but it obviously means to speak under inspiration at the least. There is an effect when one speaks with authority or inspiration. Hearts will be convicted, encouraged, and edified; the acknowledgement that God is in the midst will be made. Otherwise, if one is speaking as a scribe there will be no real change. One may say "That was a good message" but in two weeks it will be forgotten and there will be no change in the life.

Prayer: *Father, I pray that You put Your words in the mouth of those leaders that You have placed in responsibility for my spiritual growth. I ask that You bring them to a closer relationship with You so that they may receive words from heaven that have authority and not just speak as mere men.*

The Weekly Word - Week 34
Praying For Leaders (Part 4)

A third reason for praying for spiritual leaders is that they might live a life of honorable conduct. The writer of Hebrews makes this request *"Pray for us; for we are confident that we have a good conscience, in all things desiring to live honorably"* (Heb. 13:18). "In a day when dishonourable conduct is lauded and applauded, when actions of evil are rewarded while actions of righteousness are punished, when unrighteousness is continually before the eyes of the unsanctified believer, there needs to be a standard of living upheld and displayed by the leaders of the Church at large, and of the local church, to offset the flood of filth that is already covering the face of the earth."[1] The leaders of the Church, and local church, are on the frontlines of the battle against our enemy. We are told to put on the whole armor of God for a reason - we are at war.

During the past two decades we have heard of ministers who have entered into dishonourable conduct which has resulted in wounding many saints and defaming the name of Jesus. With the saints praying for their spiritual leaders the darts of the enemy can be deflected as the leaders are able to hold up their shield of faith against these attacks. Types of darts that leaders may have to defend against are insecurity, frailty, frustration, envy, competitiveness, strife, debate, helplessness and ungodly desires. The prayers of the saints can give strength to the leaders so they can continue to hold up their hands in the day of battle. Even as Aaron and Hur held up the hands of Moses, the saints of God must hold up the hands of their leaders with prayer.

One of the worst sins a leader can enter into is idolatry. This occurs when a minister begins to think of himself as something he is not. *"For I say, through the grace given to me, to everyone who is among you, not to think of himself more highly than he*

1 Holding Up Their Hands, Authorhouse, p. 39-40; c 2009, Terrance Kuhn

ought to think, but to think soberly, as God has dealt to each one a measure of faith" (Rom. 12:3). Our enemy tempts everyone, especially ministers, with thinking highly of themselves.

This was the case with the Pharisee Saul as he went about to destroy those who were part of "The Way". God was merciful with Saul and interrupted his life by knocking him off from his high horse named "Pride" and blinding him. When a person begins to think more of himself than what is true he becomes blind to reality. The saints of God cannot allow this to happen to their leaders. The word of God tells us "*I dwell on a high and holy place, and also with the contrite and lowly of spirit in order to revive the spirit of the lowly and to revive the heart of the contrite*" (Is. 57:15). The word revive in this passage can mean to keep, make alive, preserve, or restore to life. When God revives a person he replaces that person's viewpoint of himself and others with God's viewpoint of him or her.

When the man or woman of God sees himself or herself the way God sees him or her, he can have a good conscience to live with. God makes this plea with mankind, "*Heaven is My throne, and the earth is My footstool. Where then is a house you could build for Me? And where is a place that I may rest? For My hand made all these things, thus all these things came into being,*" declares the LORD. "*But to this one I will look, to him who is humble and contrite of spirit, and who tremble at My word*" (Is. 66:1, 2). It is not enough for a man to think of himself in a certain way because of what he has accomplished, as Saul did. The leaders of the church must see themselves as God sees them and the prayers of the saints can be a powerful tool to bring this to pass.

Prayer: *Lord God, I pray that my spiritual leaders live a life of honorable conduct at all times. As I help to hold up their hands in the day of battle, give them the awareness of tricks of the devil coming against them. I ask that You help them to always put their eyes upon You for the life they are to live.*

The Weekly Word - Week 35
Demonstration or Words

In John 13:15-16 Jesus says, *"For I have given you an example that you should do as I have done to you. Verily, verily, I say unto you, the servant is not greater than his master; neither is he that is sent greater than the one who sent him."* It is very important that teaching is done by example rather than simply by word of mouth. The apostle Paul encouraged Timothy to be an example, *"Let no one look down on your youthfulness, but rather in speech, conduct, love, faith, and purity, show yourself an example of those who believe"* (1 Tim. 4:12). The lifestyle of a follower of Christ is being seen of all men; discerned by all men; judged by all men. Every believer must strive to be an example to all who read his or her life. This is especially important in the area of healing and deliverance, or miracles.

In the gospel according to Mark 1:23-27 we find the account where Jesus went into the synagogue and a man with an unclean spirit recognized him and began to manifest. The Lord simply said, *"Be quiet, and come out of him."* The unclean spirit then threw the man into convulsions, cried out loudly, and left the man. *"And they were all amazed, so that they debated among themselves, saying, "What is this? A new teaching with authority! He commands even the unclean spirits, and they obey Him."* The teaching concerning casting out, and having authority over, demons was not verbally communicated to the people. It was simply demonstrated before the people. The people called the demonstration of having authority over demons to be a "new teaching".

When the Lord sent out the twelve disciples He gave them these instructions, *"Heal the sick, raise the dead, cleanse the leper, cast out demons; freely you have received, freely give"* (Mat. 10:8). The Lord didn't sit the apostles down and give them a course on "Casting out Demons" He just told them to do it. He had the authority and He gives that authority to us.

In the illustration above the man with the unclean spirit first came to Jesus, saying, *"What do we have to do with You, Jesus of Nazareth? Have you come to destroy us? I know who You are - the Holy One of God!"* (v. 24) The Lord did not start this confrontation, the demons did. It is interesting that the unclean spirits asked Jesus if He had come to destroy them because when the Lord received His commission He read, *"He has sent Me to proclaim release to the captives"* (Lk 4:18). Jesus did come to destroy the unclean habitations of demons. And now He sends us to do the same thing in His stead. But today there is more fear than faith in the average, or sub average, believer because they do not know the authority that has been given to them.

What is the importance of walking in the authority given to us by the Lord? Mark 1:28 reads, *"And immediately the news about Him went out everywhere into all the surrounding district of Galilee."* As soon as the Lord displayed His power over unclean spirits He became a magnate to those who needed help. The Lord spoke in this manner regarding the Kingdom, *"But if I cast out demons by the Spirit of God, then the Kingdom of God has come unto you,"* (Mat. 12:28). When an unclean spirit is cast out of a person the Kingdom of God is displayed on earth. When the Lord went about on His evangelistic road, *"He went into their synagogues throughout all Galilee, preaching and casting out the demons"* (Mk 1:39). The Lord did not need to go out into the streets to find demons they were already in the house of worship; brought in by people. And so they are today. The demons just need to be identified and then the people can be set free.

When one has too much false humility they will be no use to the Kingdom. The attitude of "I do not want to be seen" does the Kingdom no good. Saints cannot hide under a bushel; they we must be a light. *"Let your light shine before men in such a way that they may see your good works and glorify your Father who is in heaven"* (Mat. 5:16). In this verse people see you but glorify God. We must freely preach the gospel and display the Kingdom of God bringing the Kingdom to earth.

Prayer: *Lord Jesus, I desire to display the Kingdom of God on earth just as You did. You brought the Kingdom with power and not just by words. I ask that You build my faith that I might exercise the power of the Kingdom and not just speak the Word of the Kingdom.*

The Weekly Word - Week 36
The Pattern To Build

In this era of high technology and fast paced society we often neglect to search out the proper pattern that the LORD gave us to build His Church. Such also has been the case with the proper pattern for the reproduction of leaders in the local church and Church worldwide. This is especially true in the leading nations of the world where the education of our church leaders has been delegated to universities and theological seminaries where many go in on fire for God and come out in a coffin. This was not the pattern set forth by God and our spiritual forefathers. When Moses led the people of Israel out of Egypt a young man by the name of Joshua was chosen by God, attached himself to Moses, learned from him, was set apart by the laying on of hands, and became the leader of Israel after Moses' death.

As we fast-forward to the end days of the Old Testament we find the Lord Jesus Christ choosing twelve disciples to whom He would pour out Himself and equip to further His ministry once He ascended into heaven. These twelve disciples did not only receive the general teachings that Jesus gave but they received special training and equipping in a more intimate setting. They did not all have the same personality or the same special qualities in order to be chosen. They were simply born of like spirit with a desire to serve the one who chose them - Jesus.

This same pattern is found in the lives of Paul and Peter; two apostles who gave birth to sons. Paul had at least two sons, Timothy and Titus, and Peter had at least one son - John Mark. Of these three we can observe a trail of growth in the life of Titus. In the epistle to Titus Paul wrote, *"For this reason I left you in Crete, that you might set in order what remains, and appoint elders in every city as I directed you,"*(Titus 1:5). Titus, a spiritual son of Paul, was given the responsibility to complete the setting in order the leadership of those churches in Crete that Paul had initially established. Prior to receiving this responsibility, however, there was a road that Titus journeyed, approving himself of being worthy of becoming an apostle.

In chronological order the first time we hear of Titus is in Galatians 2:3 (see Acts 15) when Paul and Barnabus present themselves before the council in Jerusalem regarding the question of circumcision. *"But not even Titus, who was with me, though he was a Greek, was compelled to be circumcised."* The council in Jerusalem took place around 51 A.D. when Titus was approximately 39 years old.

We then find Titus doing an apostolic work among the Corinthian church in Paul's third letter to the Corinthian church, *"Consequently we urged Titus that as he previously had made a beginning, so also he would complete in you this gracious work as well"* (2 Cor. 8:6). Evidently, Titus helped to begin a work in Corinth, had been sent somewhere else, and had returned. When he returned he was refreshed to hear the news pertaining to the progress that the Corinthian church had achieved. He also was highly spoken of by Paul, *"But thanks be to God, who puts the same earnestness on your behalf in the heart of Titus. For he not only accepted our appeal, but being himself very earnest, he has gone to you of his own accord"* (2 Cor. 8:16-17). During his time of training under the tutelage of Paul, Titus had shown his desire, affection, and trustworthiness. At a later time, Paul sent Titus back to Corinth to continue serving the Corinthian church. (2 Cor. 12:18)

In 2 Timothy 4:10 we find Paul requesting Timothy to come to him because the apostolic team had been so diminished and Titus had gone to Dalmatia. At some time there had been a regrouping and Paul leaves Titus in Crete, not far from Corinth, to establish the Church in every city. The last thing that Paul says to Titus is, *"When I send Artemas or Tychucus to you, make every effort to come to me at Nicopolis, for I have decided to spend the winter there"* (Tit. 3:12).

Titus had learned from Paul, received the same heart for the church that Paul had, had been sent out to help establish churches and had returned, and finally was given the opportunity and responsibility to establish churches himself with the help of others, becoming a spiritual son to Paul. Titus' education was based on relationship to one who could "father" him in the faith and was not based on mere book learning.

Prayer: *Lord God, bring people to the leaders of the church that they might prepare them for the works of service as You have designed in Your word. Place an anointing upon those You have chosen to continue the work of the ministry to the saints of God and to the world.*

The Weekly Word - Week 37
Timothy

The second spiritual son that we can study is Timothy. Timothy was very close to Paul, and Paul included him on some of his apostolic ventures. *"Paul, an apostle of Christ Jesus by the will of God, and Timothy our brother, to the church of God which is in Corinth with all the saints who are throughout Achaia: Grace to you and peace from God our Father and the Lord Jesus Christ"* (2 Cor. 1:1-2). In Paul's epistle to the Corinthians he includes Timothy as if he were writing it also, like a coauthor. As with Titus, Paul took Timothy through an equipping period of ministering to different churches before leaving him in Ephesus *"in order that you may instruct certain men not to teach strange doctrines, nor to pay attention to myths and endless genealogies, which give rise to mere speculation rather than furthering the administration of God which is by faith"* {1 Tim. 1:3-4).

In total there are 19 references of Timothy in the records written by Luke, Paul, and the writer of Hebrews. Luke mentions Timothy as being a disciple of Christ and a helper to Paul, as a deacon. Timothy and others were attendants to Paul as he walked his apostolic journeys. But Paul equipped them, as Jesus did, to do the work of the ministry. Paul speaks of Timothy as being a coworker, messenger, son, apostle, brother, fellow preacher, coauthor, brother, and fellow laborer. And the writer of Hebrews mentions Timothy as being a brother (Heb. 13:23)

The relationship between Paul and Timothy begins in Lystra where Paul meets Timothy where the brethren speak very well of Timothy and Paul decided he *"wanted to have him go on with him"* (Ac 16:3). There are many times in the ministry of Paul where we can see him following the pattern of Jesus in bringing people into their destiny. Paul takes Timothy, as well as others, to help preach in every city *"the decrees to keep, which were determined by the apostles and elders at Jerusalem"* (v.4). In addition, Timothy ministered to Paul prior to being sent out on his own apostolic escapades. (Ac 19:22)

As Paul journeyed on his apostolic route through Greece he took many younger ministers with him. *"And Sopater of Berea accompanied him in Asia- also Aristarchus and Secundus of the Thessalonians, and Gaius of Derbe, and Timothy, and Tychicus and Trophimus of Asia"* (Ac 20:4). As Paul would mentor these men he would have them journey out for a time and then return. *"So he sent into Macedonia two of those who ministered to him, Timothy and Erastus, but he himself stayed in Asia for a time"* (Ac 19:22). A second example is found in Col. 4:7-9, *"Tychicus, a beloved brother, faithful minister (deacon, teacher, pastor), and fellow servant in the Lord, will tell you all the news about me. I am sending him to you for this very purpose, that he may know your circumstances and comfort your hearts, with Onesimus, a faithful and beloved brother, who is one of you."* (parenthesis authors)

In 1st Timothy 1:3 we see where Paul leaves Timothy in Ephesus *"that you may charge some that they teach no other doctrine, nor give heed to fables or endless genealogies, which cause dispute rather than godly edification which is in faith."* Two years later Paul writes to Timothy from Rome and tells him to come to him for he is soon to depart this world. Timothy had gone through a process of being taught, equipped, internship, and finally receiving his own apostleship. Paul continued to stay in contact with his son in the faith encouraging him to preach the truth. Paul took the lead and the initiative with his son Timothy to bring him into his destiny.

The Weekly Word - Week 38
John Mark

The final "spiritual son" that we are going to look at is John Mark. The word of God convinces me that each person in leadership must look for those who might become sons or daughters in the faith and begin to transform their lives through personal relationship. I believe that this must be of utmost importance. Most leaders probably have "mentored" others but bringing up sons and daughters goes much further. After a long difficult road John Mark became the "spiritual son" to Peter. *"She who is in Babylon, elect together with you, greets you; and so does Mark my son"* (1 Pet. 5:13).

We initially meet Mark in Acts 12:12 as Peter is set free from jail by an angel of God. Peter arrives at the house of Mary *"the mother of John whose surname was Mark, where many were gathered together praying."* At this same time the church in Antioch decided to send financial support to the church in Jerusalem by the hands of Barnabus and Saul. When Barnabus and Saul had accomplished their task they returned to Antioch with John Mark who was the cousin to Barnabus (Acts 12:25; Col. 4:10). Often times a leader will see an anointing on a relative much easier than on another brother or sister because of the close relationship and bond that is already established and this should not be neglected. So Saul and Barnabus take John Mark along with them. But something happens. The apostolic life becomes too great for John Mark and he deserts Paul and Barnabus, returning to Antioch. Mark had made it to Salamis, the capital of Cyprus, and crossed over to Paphos on the opposite side of Cyprus and sailed to Perga in Pamphylia on the north shore of the Mediterranean Sea. But at this point Mark, for some unknown reason, left Paul and Barnabus.

Upon the return of Paul and Barnabus to Antioch they met with the church, again teaching and preaching the word of the Lord. Paul and Barnabus had been sent from Jerusalem with the decision of the council concerning the law which *"some of our number to whom we gave no instruction have disturbed you with their words, unsettling your souls"* (Acts 15:24). It is very important that apostles give correct instruction concerning the Word of God to sons and daughters before they are sent out to do the work of ministry. Otherwise, all kinds of things can be taught and cause "unsettling". So Paul, Barnabus, Judas, and Silas carry the Jerusalem decision to Antioch.

After a time Paul desires to return to the cities *"in which we have proclaimed the word of the Lord, and see how they are"* (Acts 15:36). Barnabus desired to take his cousin John Mark along but Paul refused because of the earlier desertion. So now John Mark goes with Barnabus to Cyprus and Paul takes Silas to Syria and Cilicia *"strengthening the churches"* (Acts 15:37 - 41). Now Mark is not only receiving instructions concerning the proper distribution of the Word of the Lord but he is going forth in his early ministry doing what he is called to do.

In his letter to the Colossians Paul instructs the saints in Colosse to welcome Mark if he comes to them (4:10). John Mark is no longer a student to Barnabus, he is now fulfilling the course that Jesus had called him to run and is a leader and Paul now calls him a fellow worker for the Kingdom of God(Col 4:11).

From what we can determine from scripture Barnabas trained, or mentored John Mark, but Peter acknowledges him as a son, *"She who is in Babylon, chosen together with you, sends you greetings, and so does my son, Mark"* (1 Pet. 5:13). As the apostle Paul wrote, *"For if you were to have countless tutors in Christ, yet you would not have many fathers; for in Christ Jesus I became your father, through the gospel"* (1 Cor. 4:15).

Prayer: *Father, I ask that You raise up Fathers who will In turn raise up sons and daughters that Your Kingdom will properly be positioned and presented to the world.*

The Weekly Word - Week 39
New Authority

Since 2012 we have seen a new season in which the Lord has been extending the authority of His apostles and those moving in apostolic anointings. In recent years many saints have had prophecies to *"enlarge the place of your tent"* (Is. 54:2) and those words have been sent forth to prepare an apostolic people for what the LORD has in store for His Church in this new season. The LORD has seen many of His called, chosen, and anointed ministers leave His service for various reasons. The least of which is the lack of proper spiritual covering that can move them into the course God has for them. But the Lord says, *"I have been dealing with hearts. I have been working in those trapped by denominational boundaries and I am about to release them from the walls of captivity. They will come forth and look for new leaders that they can grasp onto for a time to get refreshed and strengthened and they will look for apostolic leaders to impart unto them the gifts that I have for them."* Some will come out of the denominational structure; yet, some will stay in their denomination and breathe new life into those structures. And the Lord says to apostolic leaders *"Seek out new relationships with those within denominational structures for they are looking for you. For I am going to put down the reproach that many have held against My apostles and they will be freed from the understanding of the past that they have held unto."*

Many have celebrated the lives and ministries of Peter and Paul in the New Testament but little has been said about Barnabas who was a strong apostle himself. Barnabas became an apostle, and father, to Paul when many questioned Paul's conversion and were afraid of him because he once persecuted the Church. We initially see Barnabas in Acts 4:36-37, *"And Joseph, a Levite of Cyprian birth, who was also called Barnabus by the apostles (which translated means son of encouragement),* *and who owned a tract of land, sold it and brought the money* *and laid it at the apostles feet."* This description of Barnabas is very important. We are told that he was a Levite and yet he owned land. When the children of Israel inherited the Promised Land the Levites were given no land because the LORD was to be their inheritance. The Lord Jesus instructed His apostles to go forth thus, *"Take nothing for your journey, neither a staff,* *nor a bag, nor bread, nor money; and do not even have two tu-* *nics apiece"* (Lk 9:3). In his understanding of the instructions of Jesus, Barnabas sold all that he had and laid the money *"at the* *apostles' feet".* (Acts 4:37)

Barnabas is spoken of as a prophet in Acts 13:1 and then as an apostle in Acts 14:4. In Acts 9:27 he takes Paul before the apostles and communicates the events surrounding Paul's salvation to them. When some tried to put Paul to death the brethren sent him to Tarsus. After the persecution that arose in connection with Stephen, and the dispersion that followed the apostles sent Barnabas to Antioch and he encouraged the church at Antioch *"to remain true to the Lord"* (Acts 11:23). Then Barnabas went to Tarsus to look for Saul and when he found him he took him to Antioch. *"And it came about that for an entire year they* *met with the church, and taught considerable numbers; and the* *disciples were first called Christians in Antioch"* (Acts 11:26). The "word" says "they taught" not "Paul taught". So, Barnabas was teaching in Antioch and Paul was learning and Paul was also teaching. Here we see Paul being mentored by Barnabas. We next see them separated unto a course of ministry together; Paul and his apostle Barnabas. The days have come when the apostles will seek and be sought after.

Prayer*: Father, I ask that You bring apostolic authority,* *correct apostolic authority to Your people in this day and this* *hour. Your Church has struggled for so long, being without cor-* *rect apostolic covering. Lord, I ask that You bring connections* *between shepherds and apostles that Your Church would be* *strengthened.*

The Weekly Word - Week 40
Return To Repentance

The writer of Hebrews informs us that the first principle of the doctrine of Christ is "repentance from dead works" (Heb 6:1). The preaching of true repentance, bringing forth conversion, has been lacking in the 21st century Church as a whole. The formula has become to preach the second principle, faith towards God, before the preaching of repentance. The result being that not only individuals, but entire churches are living in sin, as is exemplified by the 7 churches in the Revelation of Jesus Christ.

A study of the ministry of John the Baptist shows that he preached repentance first, "*Repent, for the Kingdom of heaven is at hand*" (Mt. 3:2). He followed these words with "*Make ready the way of the LORD, make His paths straight*" (Mat 3:3). The first command John speaks "*make ready the way of the LORD*" is in the aorist imperative tense which means it is a simple action which only needs to be done once. The second command "*make His paths straight*" is in the present imperative tense meaning it involves continuous or repeated action. This is explained as John tells the Pharisees and Sadducees "*to bring fruit in keeping with repentance*" (Mat 3:8).

A person makes "*ready the way of the LORD*" with initial repentance of living a lifestyle contrary to the "way" of the LORD. A "way" is a road or a route that shows progress being made in a person's life; that the person is now starting a new journey. The second phrase that John speaks tells the listener that the road that has been worn down or made into a rut must be replaced with walking a level road.

Jesus begins His ministry with the same command, "*Repent, for the Kingdom of heaven is at hand*" (Mat 4:17). Here the word "repent" is also in the present imperative tense meaning it involves continuous or repeated action. Repentance is not to be used just as a means of feeling good but as a means of being cleansed of known sin and to change the journey one is on.

Repentance is pictured in the Tabernacle of Moses as the Levites were to give a sacrifice both morning and evening as a continual offering at the door of the tabernacle where God said He would meet with them(Ex. 29:39-42). This sacrifice is, therefore, a picture of our worship of God. The act of true repentance is a form of worship. Jesus followed this command with *"You shall not commit adultery, you shall not steal, you shall not bear false witness"* (Mat 19:18). Jesus tells us that we must change; we must be converted, in our way of living. Then Jesus says, *"There is no good tree which produces bad fruit; nor, on the other hand, a bad tree which produces good fruit. For each tree is known by its own fruit"* (Mat 6:43-44).

A third illustration of the importance of repentance is given to us by Paul, an apostle, as he pleads his case to king Agrippa, *"I did not prove disobedient to the heavenly vision, but kept declaring truth to those of Damascus first, and also at Jerusalem, and then throughout all the region of Judea, and even to the Gentiles that they should repent and turn to God performing deeds appropriate to repentance"* (Acts 26:19-20). As did John and Jesus, Paul states that repentance is the initial act that must be performed in order to change the journey one is walking.

We conclude than that true repentance is not just the mouthing of words showing sorrow but it involves actions which prove there has been a true conversion. As Paul wrote to the church in Ephesus, *"Let him that stole steal no longer, but rather let him labor, working with his hands what is good,"* (Eph 5:28). As the heavenly vision was shown unto Paul so must we preach, *"I will deliver you from the Jewish people, as well as from the Gentiles, to whom I now send you, to open their eyes, in order to turn them from darkness to light, and from the power of Satan to God, that they may receive forgiveness of sins and an inheritance among those who are sanctified by faith in Me"* (Acts 26:16- 18).

Prayer: *Lord, I ask that the truth be spoken from my lips and that repentance be preached first whenever I preach salvation to one who is lost. I also ask that my motives be pure in Your sight and that You give me the words to speak that the hearer might be saved.*

The Weekly Word - Week 41
Compassion

Much has been spoken concerning the need for each believer to abide in faith, hope, and love. Volumes of teaching have been given in the past 30 years on the need to walk in faith to the extent that faith has been trampled into the ground. But little has been mentioned as to the need for each saint of God to walk in compassion as Peter wrote *"Finally, be ye all of one mind, having compassion one of another, love as brethren, be pitiful, be courteous: not rendering evil for evil, or railing for railing: but contrariwise blessing: knowing that ye are thereunto called, that ye should inherit a blessing"* (1 Pet 3:8-9, NKJV). The New American Standard Bible renders verse 8, *"To sum up, let all be harmonious, sympathetic, brotherly, kindhearted, and humble in spirit."* Verse 8 speaks of how disciples, members of the body of Christ, are to treat one another.

Peter tells us to be compassionate, or sympathetic, towards one another and to refrain from speaking evil or guile of one another, seeking peace. The Greek word translated compassion is *"soom-path-ace'* "which specifically means *"having a fellow-feeling"* and is only used twice in scripture. The word comes from *"soom-pas-kho"* meaning *"to experience pain jointly, or of the same kind, specifically persecution."* This action is spoken of in Romans 12:15-16, *"Rejoice with those who rejoice; and weep with those who weep. Be of the same mind toward one another."*

Paul further explains this thought in Romans 8:16-17, *"The Spirit Himself bears witness with our spirit that we are children of God, and if children, heirs with Christ, if indeed we suffer with Him in order that we also may be glorified with Him,"* and also in 1 Cor. 12:25-26, *"there should be no division in the body, but that the members should have the same care for one another.*

And if one member suffers, all the members suffer with it; if one member is honored, all the members rejoice with it." The heart of the matter is that God wants our hearts to be knit together one with another; we are to share suffering as well as rejoicing.

When we look at one another with eyes of compassion we will be able to realize another's pain or experience their struggle. As we experience this fellow-feeling, God can give us wisdom, understanding, or authority to deal with the matter. This compassion will also allow us to authentically experience jointly the suffering being felt.

As seen previously soom-path-ace' is used in 1 Peter 3:8. The other time it is used is in 1 John 3:17, "*But whoever has this world's goods, and beholds his brother in need and closes his heart against him, how does the love of God abide in him?*" Both of these scriptures speak about how we are to treat our brothers and sisters in Christ. Sadly, the Church as a whole has more compassion for the world than she does for her own members. As we see members of the body being afflicted naturally or spiritually we must come alongside them and give comfort, support, or deliverance as we are enabled by the Lord Jesus Christ through compassion.

Prayer: *Father, fill me with compassion that I might walk with my brothers and sisters in Christ in their time of need, sharing their pain and suffering.*

The Weekly Word Week 42
Kings and Priests

John, the apostle, writes in The Revelation of Jesus Christ that the Lord Jesus *"has made us kings and priests to His God and Father"* (Rev. 1:6). It is very important that we understand the position that we have in relationship to God, the Father, and for that matter to the world. We are first made kings, those that rule, those that are sovereign. The Greek word translated "kings" is *basileuo* meaning "to rule". Jesus, the sovereign King, has set us upon a rock not upon quicksand. The foundation on which we stand is one of power over our enemies that we can reign in this life.

When Solomon was made king by the will of God he asked *"Now give me wisdom and knowledge, that I may go out and come in before this people; for who can judge this great people of Yours?"* (2 Chr. 1:10) Solomon asked God for the same ability that He had given Moses when Moses led the people of Israel, for God had given Moses wisdom to judge the people. *"And it came to pass on the morrow that Moses sat to judge the people: and the people stood by Moses from the morning unto the evening"* (Exo. 18:13). The word judge means to "pronounce sentence for or against; to vindicate or punish." The people of God need to be able to discern good from evil; what is right and what is wrong; what is godly and what is worldly.

As we walk this life as strangers in a strange land we must consider ourselves to be *"more than conquerors through Him who loved us"* (Rom. 8:27). I am reminded of the movie "The Day the Earth Stood Still" where they could not destroy the alien visitor. As we read the list of those included in the Hall of Fame of Faith in Hebrews the passage records this about them, *"These all died in faith, not having received the promises, but having seen them afar off were assured of them, embraced them and*

confessed that they were strangers and pilgrims on the earth."
(Heb. 11:13) The Hall of Fame is still taking members and I
want to be included. How about you? Through Him who loves
us we can do all things.

As priests we are to take the many prayer requests that we
have received and offer them to God as a sweet smelling aroma,
without doubt. Within the inner court of the Tabernacle of Moses stood the altar of incense. It is here where we offer up our
prayers to God and act as intercessors for the world, "*And the
smoke of the incense, with the prayers of the saints, ascended
before God from the angel's hand*" (Rev. 8:4). We are told in
Romans 8:26-27 that the Spirit makes intercession for us, the
saints of God. In turn, we are to make intercession to God for
the world. Thus, we are priests unto God offering prayers as
incense to God, praying for those caught in the trap of the devil.
We are both kings and priests to God.

Prayer: *As a king and a priest unto You, O Lord, I ask that
I be given the understanding that I need to walk in those positions. As a king, I am a ruler on this earth; ruling over sin and
circumstances. As a priest I am a servant to all mankind offering prayers that You would intervene on their behalf. I thank
You, Lord, that my position is in Christ, no longer in the world,
where I can rule and reign with my King.*

The Weekly Word - Week 43
From Shittim to Gilgal (Part 1)

In Micah 6:5 the LORD tells Israel to remember three historical events. First, He tells them to remember Balak who attempted to persuade Balaam to prophesy against Israel with the means of monetary wealth. Secondly, Israel is told to remember Balaam who wanted desperately to prophesy against Israel for gain *"because he loved the wages of wickedness"* (2 Pet 2:15) but could not and was rebuked by a donkey.

Third, Israel was told to *"remember your journey from Shittim to Gilgal"* which was simply took Israel from the east side of Jordan to the west side of Jordan. They were told to remember these three things *"that you may know the righteousness of the LORD."* If one was to look at a coin as an analogy of the nature of God compassion and mercy would be on one side and righteousness and truth would be on the other side. Grace and mercy must be balanced.

There were many events which occurred while Israel was camped at Acacia Grove (Shittim) on the east side of the Jordan in Moab across from Gilgal. The entire episode between Balak and Balaam occurred here and Israel committed much sin at Shittim. *"Now Israel remained in Shittim, and the people began to commit harlotry with the women of Moab. They invited the people to the sacrifice's of their gods, and the people ate and bowed down to their* gods" (Num. 25:1-2). Idolatry is a great offense to the LORD and according to His direction Moses commanded the judges of Israel, *"each one of you slay his men who joined themselves to Baal of Peor"* (Num. 25:5). Since the LORD cannot allow sin to continue and be manifest among His people His righteousness had to be displayed.

During the "crossing over" Jordan to Gilgal there were also three important acts of God that occurred. First, as soon as the

Ark of the Covenant entered the waters of Jordan the waters were cut off, just as they had been in the incident of the Red Sea, to allow the children of Israel to pass through the water. Second, as soon as the Ark of the Covenant came from the river bed onto dry land the waters returned to their original height. Third, great fear entered into the hearts of the Amorite and Canaanite kings (Ex. 5:1).

There was something else that Joshua was instructed to do as they crossed over the Jordan. He was told to have twelve men, one from each tribe, gather twelve stones from the river and he stacked them at Gilgal as a testimony that the hand of the LORD is with Israel. There were also twelve stones placed in the midst of the Jordan for the twelve priests to have a firm footing as the people passed over.

As the number twelve speaks of governmental authority, the LORD is giving us an insight into the necessity of standing on a firm foundation. In the New Testament we read *"Now, therefore, you are no longer strangers and foreigners, but fellow citizens with the saints and members of the household of God, having been built on the foundation of the apostles and prophets, Jesus Christ Himself being the chief cornerstone, in whom the whole building, being fitted together, grows into a holy temple in the Lord, in whom you also are being built together for a dwelling place of God in the Spirit"* (Eph. 2:19-22). The twelve stones that Joshua put in the river and the twelve stones he stacked in Gilgal both symbolized the need the Church has for the foundation to be layed by apostles and prophets.

Prayer: *Lord, I am beginning to understand the need for the Church as a whole, and each local church, to be firmly standing on the foundation of the apostles and prophets, as they are extension ministries of Jesus Himself. As we cross over from Shittim to Gilgal I ask that You place the right foundation under my feet that I do not slip and that I might always stand on a firm foundation.*

The Weekly Word - Week 44
Crossing Over Jordan

When Israel crossed over the Jordan there were two spiritual ceremonies that were conducted - circumcision and Passover. Every male who had been born in Egypt had been circumcised but those who had been born in the wilderness had not been circumcised; for forty years no male had been circumcised.

Circumcision is the sign of the covenant between man and God and is very important to God (Jos. 5:4-5). In the New Testament, when one turns to God from following his own ways he is spiritually circumcised by the Holy Spirit, in heart, allowing him or her to enter into a position where he can legally take part in and receive the Passover of God. When the people of Israel had all been circumcised God *"rolled away the reproach of Egypt"* (Jos. 5:9) from off them. When they were circumcised to the LORD the disgrace and the shame of Egypt was taken off from them. Now that they were circumcised they could freely partake of the LORD's Passover. God tells us to *"Circumcise yourselves to the LORD, and take away the foreskins of your hearts, you men of Judah and inhabitants of Jerusalem, lest My fury come forth like fire, and burn so that no one can quench it, because of the evil of your doings"* (Jer. 4:4). We must be circumcised unto the LORD in order to walk in covenant with our God. Without a person's heart being circumcised that person cannot enter into covenant with God.

The children of Israel celebrated the Passover on the 14th day of the first month, Abib. This was the day that God had prescribed for Israel to celebrate the Passover when they first came out from Egypt. Today, the uncircumcised, the world, has dictated to the Church that the Passover be celebrated based on the first full moon after the spring equinox and they have renamed it after their fertility goddess Estra, or Estarte. Sadly, the Church has fallen into line and followed this practice.

The day after celebrating Passover the children of Israel began to eat the fruit of the land. The heavens were closed and the heavenly manna stopped. Thankfully, the Lord Jesus is our manna from heaven, *"Your fathers ate the manna in the wilderness, and they died. This is the bread that comes down out of heaven, so that one may eat it and not die"* (Jn 6:49 - 50). We are told to *"taste and see that the Lord is good"* (Ps. 34:8). The word of God also instructs us that His words are sweeter than honey to our mouth, *"How sweet are Thy words to my taste! Yes, sweeter than honey to my mouth"* (Ps. 119:103).

Jesus told us that unless we eat of His flesh and drink of His blood that we have nothing to do with Him. This does not just speak of the taking of communion (Passover supper) as a tradition, but living a life in submission to His ways. When we do partake of Him we move from glory to glory (*dignity or honor*) that *"you may know the righteous acts of the LORD"* just as the children of Israel did. When we know, when we consider, the righteous acts of God in our hearts we can than increase in faith and perform the righteous acts of God.

When the children of Israel crossed over Jordan they had already been given a vision of what was ahead of them by the two spies that had been sent ahead of them by Joshua to spy out Jericho. One might say that Gilgal was a suburb of Jericho as it lies just to the east of Jericho so the people of Jericho knew they were in trouble. The two spies were hidden by a harlot and this was her confession, *"I know that the LORD has given you the land, that the terror of you has fallen on us, and that all the inhabitants of the land are fainthearted because of you"* (Jos. 2:9).

There are several points in this last paragraph to deal with. The children of Israel had the two spies to inform them of what was ahead of them. We have the Holy Spirit and the Word of God to lead us. The men of Jericho came to find the spies to take them to the king. Often times the people of this world would desire to do harm to the saints of God but they are hidden by either the Holy Spirit or by sin that blinds men's eyes. God has a destiny to fulfill and that is to capture all of the land for His glory. Rahab, whose name means arrogance, hid the spies and even lied to protect them because the people of Jericho had become fainthearted and terror had fallen on them because of Israel. There is a day coming when terror will fill the hearts of all mankind and God says, *"Indeed I will make those of the synagogue of Satan, who say they are Jews and are not, but lie - indeed I will make then come and worship before your feet, and to know that I have loved you"* (Rev. 3:9). There is a time when the people of this world will fear the Israel of God (Church) when the Church puts on righteousness and holiness and walks before God in humility.

Prayer: *Father, I ask that You circumcise my heart anew unto You and Your Church afresh that She may walk in covenant relationship with You.*

The Weekly Word - Week 45
Team Ministry

Micah 6:4 reads, *"I brought you up out of Egypt and redeemed you from the land of slavery. I set Moses to lead you, also Aaron and Miriam."* In the 21st century one might say, *"I brought you up out of the sinful world and redeemed you from the bondage of sin."* Believers are aware that our old nature has been crucified with Christ in order that the body of sin might be deposed, that we no longer shall be slaves to sin. *"Knowing this, that our old self was crucified with Him, that our body of sin might be done away with, that we no longer should be slaves to sin; for he who has died is freed from sin"* (Rom. 6:6 -7). Thanks to the sacrificial Lamb we are free from sin and free to praise and worship God.

The second thing God says that He brought to pass in this passage concerns leadership, *"I sent Moses to lead you. Also Aaron and Miriam."* God did not send one man to lead the children of Israel, He sent a team. He sent Moses as the apostle to set all things in order, He sent Aaron to be a prophet of God to Moses and the people *"and your brother Aaron shall be your prophet"* (Ex. 7:1), and He sent Miriam as a prophetess to lead the people in the dance and to celebrate the salvation of God which is why Miriam was judged so harshly with leprosy when she and Aaron challenged the leadership of Moses. Miriam had been given a dynamic leadership role so she received a harsher judgment. She sat as a leader of worship as did Lucifer prior to his fall from grace.

This pattern of "team leadership" is all throughout the Old Testament and the New Testament. In the Old Testament there were kings in Israel and Judah and they always had a prophet who was speaking in their hearing as to what God was saying even if they did not want to hear it. For example, Saul had

Samuel, David had Nathan and Gad, and Jeroboam had Ahijah. Even when the king did not want the prophet to speak he spoke to inform the king of the mind of God in an attempt to keep the king on the right track.

When Jesus was taken into heaven He left gifts to men as was prophesied by the psalmist in Psalms 68:18, *"Thou hast ascended on high, thou hast led captive the captives; thou hast received gifts among men, even among the rebellious also, that the LORD God may dwell there."* This prophecy is shown to be fulfilled in the New Testament Church *"But to each one of us grace was given according to the measure of Christ's gift. Therefore it says, 'When He ascended on high, He led on high a host of captives, and He gave gifts to men. And He gave some as apostles, and some as prophets, and some as evangelists, and some as pastors and teachers,'"* (Eph. 4:8, 11). The Lord did not just leave one gift to the church, He left five.

As we perform a survey of the Book of the Acts of the Apostles we find this same pattern. When Jesus ascended to the throne He left twelve apostles to watch over the church in Jerusalem and begin to branch out into other regions and nations. In Acts 3 we see Peter and John going to the temple to pray when they are confronted by a lame man from birth. Peter and John fixed their gaze upon him and Peter says, *"In the name of Jesus the Nazarene - walk"* (Acts 3:1-6). Later, in Acts 4, we see Peter and John being arrested. In Acts 5, the apostles were performing signs and wonders and many who were sick or afflicted with evil spirits were brought to the apostles and they were all healed (12-16).

Then in Acts 6 - 8 we read the accounts of two deacons, Stephen and Philip, who were preaching with much power and performing *"great wonders and signs among the people"* (Acts 6:8; 8:6). In the case of Stephen, we see where he ended up being stoned, being alone. In the case of Philip, he went forth healing the sick, casting out devils, and he brought the Ethiopian to salvation. Philip then went down to the city of Samaria preaching Jesus and many were paying attention to him. *"But when they believed Philip preaching the good news about the kingdom of God and the name of Jesus Christ, they were being baptized, men and women alike"* (Acts 8:12). But Philip could only take the people so far, *"Now when the apostles at Jerusalem heard that Samaria had received the word of God, they sent them Peter and John, who came down and prayed for them, that they might receive the Holy Spirit"* (Acts 8:15). The people in Samaria had received the Lord Jesus Christ and had been baptized of water but had not as yet received the Holy Spirit. Peter and John were needed to administer a further revelation and spiritual experience of significance through laying hands on them (v. 17) that they would receive the Holy Spirit. In this passage we once again see the importance of team ministry to advance the growth of the believer.

Prayer: *I understand that the Church as a Body and the local church as an expression of Jesus Christ needs team ministry to ignite and unite the Body of Christ. Please Father, bring the ministries together in a powerful way to equip the saints to be powerful conduits of the Holy Spirit.*

The Weekly Word - Week 46
Building the House (Haggai - Part 1)

There are times when leaders must take inventory and evaluate the condition of the sheep. That is to say that a leader must ask periodically, "Are the sheep strong, or, are they weak in the faith?" "Are they taking an active part in building the Kingdom of God or simply wanting to be built?" This malady was faced by Haggai the prophet when God revealed the hearts of the people to him, "*This people says, 'The time has not come, the time that the LORD's house should be built.'*" Then the LORD asks this question "*Is it time for you yourselves to dwell in your paneled houses, and this temple to lie in ruins?*" (Hag 1:2, 4)

God spoke this word to Haggai in the second year of king Darius which would have been 520 B.C. The decree to allow the people of Judah to go and rebuild the temple had come some 19 years earlier by Cyrus, king of Persia. A total of 42,360 men and women of Judah, 7,337 servants, and two hundred men and women singers had returned to Jerusalem to build the temple of the LORD.

In the seventh month of the second year of Cyrus king of Persia "*the people gathered together as one man to Jerusalem*" (Ezra 3:1). The first thing they did was build an altar of sacrifice to offer burnt offerings to the LORD (v.3). The altar always signifies the importance of worship and God always has worship as foundational in the life of His people. The manuscript than says that they offered burnt offerings morning and evening and kept the Feast of Tabernacles. (v.4)

"*In the second month of the second year of their coming to the house of God at Jerusalem, Zerubbabel the son of Shealtiel, Jeshua the son of Jozadak, and the rest of their brethren the priests and the Levites, and all those who had come out of*

*the captivity to Jerusalem began work and appointed the Lev-
ites from twenty years old and above to observe the work of
the house of the LORD"* (Ezra 3:8). The first thing restored in
the temple was worship. The foundation was second. *"When
the builders laid the foundation of the temple of the LORD, the
priests stood in their apparel with trumpets, and the Levites, the
sons of Asaph, with cymbals, to praise the LORD, according
to the ordinance of David king of Israel. And they sang re-
sponsively, praising and giving thanks to the LORD: 'For He is
good, for His mercy endures forever toward Israel. Then all the
people shouted with a great shout, when they praised the LORD,
because the foundation of the house of the LORD was laid"* (Ez
3:10-11). Much joy was being released because the foundation
had been laid. The worship of God had been restored to Israel
and now the foundation of the temple had been laid resulting in
great rejoicing among the people.

Trouble now came on the horizon. There were those in the
land who wanted to hinder the building of the temple. The ad-
versaries of Judah and Benjamin came to Zerubbabel and said,
"Let us build with you, for we seek your God as you do." But
Zerubbabel responded, *"You may do nothing with us to build a
house for our God; but we alone will build to the LORD God
of Israel, as King Cyrus the king of Persia has commanded us"*
(Ez. 4:3). But the people of the land did not listen and *"tried to
discourage the people of Judah. They troubled them in building
and hired counselors against them to frustrate their purpose all
the days of Cyrus king of Persia, even until the reign of Darius
king of Persia"* (Ez. 4:3-5).

This historical account shows us that building, or restoring,
the House of God is not easy. Enemies will come and desire to
frustrate the hands of those building and we must realize that we
are in a battle. Zerubbabel, a picture of the apostle, and the worship element of the temple have been restored. The foundation
has been laid, not only speaking of the manhood of the apostles
and prophets, but speaking of the character of the apostles and
prophets, correct doctrines, and most importantly Jesus Christ

being placed as the cornerstone.   The enemies of the work now begin to raise their ugly heads and attempt to infiltrate the building of the temple - the Church (each individual saint).   When Cyrus died in 530 B.C. Ahasuerus took the throne and brought forth a command to the extent that *"the work of the house of God which is at Jerusalem ceased, and it was discontinued until the second year of the reign of Darius king of Persia"* (Ez. 4:24).

it is once again time to build the temple of God, both in the individual life of each saint and within the cities in which our God desires to dwell - all of them.   The people of this world, the governments, the religious community, the atheists and agnostics have raised their ugly heads and stopped the work but it is time to cut off the heads of those who oppose God and establish His Kingdom.

Prayer: *Father, I decree, as Cyrus did, that it is time to build the temple of God once more.*

The Weekly Word - Week 47
Haggai Part 2

Continuing on with the first oracle spoken by Haggai we hear God explaining the condition of Judah, *"Consider your ways! You have sown much, but harvest little; you eat, but there is not enough to be satisfied; you drink but there is not enough to become drunk; you put on clothing, but no one is warm enough; and he who earns, earns wages to put into a purse with holes"* (Hag 1:6). Again, in verse 7 God says, *"Consider your ways!"* When God repeats a statement, He is trying to get our attention. He wants us to **"Consider our ways."** It couldn't be any plainer.

In the individual life of a person the gospel has been changed from preaching a gospel of the Kingdom, one of strength; to preaching a gospel of salvation, one of weakness. The word of God does not say that we must "Accept Jesus Christ". It tells us that a person must repent and turn to God for the Kingdom of God is near. Jesus said, *"Follow Me"* (Mk. 2:14). Many people go to Church that have never made Jesus Christ Lord and Savior of their life and many people have "accepted Jesus Christ" but have never forsaken their ways, turned to God, and began to follow Jesus.

Once again in verse 9 the LORD describes their spiritual condition, *"You look for much, but behold it comes to little; when you bring it home, I blow it away. Why?" declares the LORD of hosts, "Because of My house which lies desolate, while each of you runs to his own house."* What is God trying to tell us? In the natural He is telling us that we have put more effort and materials into building our own houses than somewhere He can dwell. In the spiritual He is telling us that we have been concerned about holding unto the past instead of looking to Him for what He is doing in the present and will do in the future. Much of the Church is too busy building monuments to those of old who had present truth vision for their time, and holding onto past revelations, that it is still busy building the past in the present. Luther, Zwingli, John Wesley, and Amy Simple McPherson are still held in esteem as if their revelations were new today. But we must build on those revelations; we must progress by using those revelations as stepping stones, not simply hold onto them.

The LORD then reproves the people of Judah for their own condition, *"Therefore, because of you the sky has withheld its dew, and the earth has withheld its produce. And I called for a drought on the land, on the mountains, on the grain, on the new wine, on the oil, on what the ground produces, on men, on cattle, and on all the labor of your hands"* (v.10-11). The Church has been asking God to "Pour the Rain" and has been rebuking the devil for the lack that it has suffered during this time. But the LORD will not send the rain, and the lack will continue until there is a humbling and repentance in the Church from walking in our own ways.

Most of us know what the LORD says in II Chronicles 7:14 for it has been preached since the early 1970's. But what does II Chronicles 7:13 say? Answer: *"If I shut up the heavens so there is no rain, or if I command the locust to devour the land, or if I send pestilence among My people"*. Then the LORD continues with verse 14, *"and if My people who are called by My name humble themselves and pray, and seek My face and turn from their wicked ways, then I will hear from heaven, will forgive their sin, and heal their land."* It is God who has closed up the heaven. It is God who has sent the locusts. It is God who has sent the pestilence because of our disobedience not the devil. We must come together as one as they did in the time of Haggai and obey the *"voice of the LORD their God and the words of Haggai the prophet, as the LORD their God had sent him. And the people showed reverence for the LORD"* (v. 12).

The Hebrew word translated as reverence in this verse is the word *yare'* pronounced yaw-ray' and it means "to fear; (moral) to revere; (causative) to frighten." What this word tells us is that when God speaks an alarming word to us, a word to get our attention such as, *"Consider your ways!"* we need to take note and come under the fear of God and seek His face and turn from our ways to His.

Installment number 3 from Haggai will be next week. This four week word of encouragement is probably to this date the most important message God has given me. I hope that none of us take it lightly.

Prayer: *Father, forgive us for not turning from our ways unto Yours. Forgive us, Father, for not having ears to hear Your words. Help us, Father, to "Consider our ways."*

The Weekly Word - Week 48
Haggai Part 3

Up to this point we have seen where a remnant of the people of Israel have left the captivity of Babylon to rebuild the Temple of the LORD according to the decree put forth by Cyrus, was then hindered by their enemies, rebuked for caring about their own houses while the House of the LORD stayed desolate bringing the people to repentance, at which time Haggai spoke once more the word of the LORD, saying, *"I am with you"* (Hag 1:13). The LORD was now telling the people of Judah and Israel who had come to Jerusalem *"as one man"* (Ezra 3:1), that their obedience had brought Him near.

The prophet Haggai is now introduced into the picture. No longer are there only worshippers and the apostle (as displayed by Zerubbabel and Joshua), there is now an apostolic/prophetic team with the entrance of Haggai. With the "word" that Haggai speaks the LORD strengthens Zerubbabel and Joshua to resume the building of the Temple. The builders and the proper elements to build the Temple, or the Church, must be brought together by the Apostles. There are apostles in many cities and counties of this nation who have been prepared for this great work. The word of the LORD is as it was in the days of Haggai, *"But now take courage, Zerubbabel,"* declares the LORD, *"take courage also Joshua son of Jehozadak, the high priest, and all you people of the land take courage,"* declares the LORD, *"and work; for I am with you,"* says the LORD of hosts (Hag. 2:4).. Paul, an apostle of Christ, wrote to the Corinthians *"According to the grace of God which was given to me, as a wise master builder I laid a foundation and another is building upon it. But let each man be careful how he builds upon it"* (I Cor 3:10).

The apostles and prophets now add the teachers to the building of the Temple. I Corinthians 12:28 tells us, *"And God has appointed in the church, first apostles, second prophets, third teachers, then miracles, then gifts of healings, helps, administrations, various kinds of tongues.*" In this list those that work miracles and healings would include evangelists, and those who perform helps and administration duties would include shepherds, today known as pastors. The building of the Temple was organized by apostles and strengthened by the word brought forth by prophets. *"When the prophets Haggai the prophet and Zechariah the son of Iddo, prophesied to the Jews who were in Judah and Jerusalem, in the name of the God of Israel, who was over them, then Zerubbabel the son of Shealtiel and Jeshua the son of Jozadak arose and began to build the house of God which is in Jerusalem; and the prophets of God were with them supporting them"* (Ezra 5:1-2). So we see that the main function of building the Temple, or the church, falls to the apostles with the prophets taking a secondary role. This is what we see with the apostolic teams sent out to build churches in every city. We have Paul and Barnabas, Paul and Silas, and Peter and John. Barnabus, Silas, and John all played a dual role as a lesser team member apostle and prophet to the stronger apostle Paul or Peter.

In the story of Haggai, once again opposition rises up against the resumption of the building of the Temple but this time Darius, the king of Persia, must submit to the decree put forth by Cyrus and Haggai pronounces, *"My Spirit is abiding in your midst; do not fear!" For thus says the LORD of hosts, "Once more in a little while, I am going to shake the heavens; and they will come with the wealth of all nations; and I will fill this house with glory,' says the LORD of host"*. (Hag 2:6-7). The LORD shakes heaven for the purpose of bringing lost souls into the Kingdom and filling His House with glory. The Church is on the precipice of a great harvest she must prepare and become as one man and build the House of God and not build separate little houses.

We are told by Paul to *"walk in a manner worthy of the calling with which you have been called, with all humility and gentleness, with patience, showing forbearance to one another in love, being diligent to preserve the unity of the Spirit, in the bond of peace"* (Eph 4:1-2). The apostles, prophets, teachers, evangelists, and shepherds are to build the Body of Christ up to the time that we all come to the oneness of the same persuasion and of the recognition of the Son of God (Ephesians 4:12-13).

The LORD is saying that He is with the apostles and prophets at this time to build the Church. To bring the body of Christ together and build a Temple, or a Church, where He can once again reside and not just visit from time to time.

Prayer: *Your word shows us that when Your people become one than You will be with us. Father, turn our hearts to the work of the Lord. Turn us to desiring to build Your house by allowing Your servants, the apostles, prophets, teachers, evangelists, and shepherds bring Your sheep, Your saints, into one house.*

The Weekly Word - Week
Haggai Part 4

The prophet Haggai continued to prophesy the word of the LORD to Zerubbabel and Joshua with these words, *"As for the promise which I made you when you came out of Egypt, My Spirit is abiding in your midst; do not fear! for thus says the LORD of hosts, 'Once more in a little while, I am going to shake the heavens and the earth, the sea also and the dry land. And I will shake all the nations; and they will come with the wealth of all nations; and I will fill this house with glory,' says the LORD of hosts"* (Hag 2:5-7). God will shake heaven and earth again for the purpose of bringing all nations into the Tabernacle of God. It is His desire that none perish and that all enter the Kingdom. The result of the heavens and the earth being shaken is that the house of the LORD will be filled with glory.

Jesus said, *"The thief comes only to steal, and kill, and destroy; I come that they might have life and might have it abundantly"* (Jn 10:10). The word abundant, from the Greek word *perissos* means superabundant in quantity and superior in quality; by implication excessive. The word abundant does not mean just a small change but a huge difference. It means turning mourning into joy, exchanging our righteousness which is as filthy rags for His righteousness unto justification, reconciliation with the Father, and life in the Holy Ghost.

For centuries there has been a gospel of salvation being preached which has taken people from a sinful nature to nothing more than feeling good. But Jesus told Nicodemus *"Truly, truly, I say to you, unless one is born of water and the Spirit, he cannot enter into the Kingdom of God"* (Jn 3"5). The preaching of the Kingdom is not only about getting people free from a life of sin but of opening a door for them to enter the Kingdom of God. Jesus said, *"But if I cast out demons by the Spirit of God, then the Kingdom of God has come upon you"* (Mt 12:28). Jesus was constantly preaching about the Kingdom, not only being saved from something but also being saved to something - the Kingdom of God replacing the kingdom of this world in a person's life.

God is going to fill His house with splendor - *"Do you not know that you are a temple of God, and that the Spirit of God dwells in you?"* (1 Cor. 3:16). Haggai declared that God's Spirit was abiding in their midst which is what He does in each of us. The writer of Hebrews speaks of heaven and earth shaking and finishes with these words, *"our God is a consuming fire"* (Heb. 12:29). This is what John the Baptist eluded to when he said that the Lord would baptize us with the Holy Spirit and fire, which would burn the chaff which is within.

As we allow the Holy Spirit to dwell within us, purifying us, the temple of God which we are will be filled with more of His glory and more nations will stream unto His Temple.

Prayer: *Lord God, You told us that You would pour out Your Spirit upon all flesh and that the Spirit would burn up all of the chaff like a refiner's fire. Lord, let this be done in my life that You would receive glory from my life.*

The Weekly Word - Week 50
The Kingdom of God

When the Lord Jesus was teaching us how to pray He commanded us to pray *"Your Kingdom come, Your will be done"* (Mat 6:13) declaring that we are to understand that the life we have without Him is vanity, worthless.   It is a necessity for us to not only enter the Kingdom of God ourselves but to welcome other people into it as well.   Concerning the Kingdom of God the Lord also told us *"The kingdom of God is not coming with signs to be observed; nor will they say, 'Look, here it is!' or 'There it is!' For behold, the kingdom of God is within you"* (Lk 17:20-21). The important truth that needs to be grasped hold of is that the Kingdom of God is inside us. Much of the structural Church is waiting for some unspecified time in the future for the Kingdom of God to show up when King Jesus stands on Mount Zion. But the Lord tells us that we have the Kingdom inside of us. So, how did it get there?

In his letter to the church in Rome Paul pens these words, *"For the kingdom of God is not eating or drinking, but righteousness, peace, and joy in the Holy Spirit"* (Rom 14:17). When a person receives the Holy Spirit, the Holy Spirit brings the Kingdom of God with Him. In addition Paul wrote, *"But we have this treasure in earthen vessels, that the surpassing greatness of the power may be of God and not from ourselves"* (2 Co 4:7) and *"For God has not given us a spirit of timidity, but of power, and love, and discipline"* (1 Tim 1:7). We find then that the Kingdom of God resides within us as we have received the gift of the Holy Spirit.   But we are told that the Kingdom resides in earthen vessels and herein lies the problem. Many saints have the Kingdom residing in them but they need to become more transparent so that the Kingdom can be revealed. Entering the Kingdom in such a manner is not easy. Luke informs us of what Paul and Barnabas preached concerning the Kingdom of God, *"Through many tribulations we must enter the Kingdom of God"* (Acts 14:22). One definition for the word tribulation is pressure, another is trouble.

Since we live in earthen vessels and not a glass vessel people cannot see what is within unless our earthen vessel becomes clear, transparent. As we are put through pressure and troubles we will become clearer and clearer so that the life of Jesus will be revealed. But the Kingdom does not just come in words. *"But I will come to you soon if the Lord wills, and I shall find out, not the words of those who are arrogant, but their power. For the kingdom of God does not consist in words, but in power"* (1 Co 4:19-20). Paul also stated, *"And my message and my preaching were not in persuasive words of wisdom, but in demonstration of the Spirit and of power"* (1 Cor. 2:4-5). As a Pharisee of Pharisees, Paul did not rely on his knowledge or his wisdom. His reliance was on the demonstration power of the Holy Spirit. Paul believed this was something important to seek after for the Lord said, *"But seek for His Kingdom, and these things shall be added to you. Do not be afraid little flock, for your Father has chosen gladly to give you the Kingdom"* (Lk 12:31-32).

The Father is glad to give us His Kingdom but He wants us to seek after it. Jeremiah 29:13 reads, *"And you will seek Me, and find Me, when you search for Me with all your heart."* The word "seek" specifically means to search out, especially in worship and prayer. God wants to give us the Kingdom but He wants us to desire it whole heartedly.

Prayer: *Father, I so much want the Kingdom of God to reside in me and to be displayed to the world through me. Lord, I ask that You help me to fully desire, and to seek for Your Kingdom with all of my heart that I might find it.*

The Weekly Word - Week 51
Sowing Seed

One of the foremost tasks that the Lord Jesus has given us is to sow seed. We have all heard the Parable of the Sower but I would like to revisit it once again. In this parable put forth by the Lord, we each can be placed as the Sower. As we cast out seed, the Word of God, before the multitudes it will land on four different types of soil. Unless we are directed to a certain place at a certain time as Philip was we do not know what the condition of the soil will be, and we need not be concerned. The parable says that the Sower cast the seed everywhere. He knew that some seed would fall on good soil, some on rocky soil, some on soil full of briars and weeds and some on hard soil where nothing could grow. In this parable, the Sower new there were four different kinds of soil. But the Sower knew the power within the seed he was sowing so the type of soil did not matter to him.

Concerning the disciples being dispersed from Jerusalem brought on by the persecution around 34-37 A.D., we read, *"Therefore, those who had been scattered went about preaching the word"* (Acts 8:4). Those who were scattered were not the apostles; those scattered were the believers who were being served and equipped by the apostles. These believers went forth preaching the word everywhere they went. Within a short amount of time they had been equipped by the apostles to do the work of ministry. They were equipped to spread the gospel of the Kingdom of God. In many churches today people hear good messages on Sunday morning or Wednesday evening but are never equipped to do the work of preaching the word or demonstrating the power of God.

There are many reasons for this result but I am going to stay focused on message. Every time a person sows the word into a heart that word is falling on one of four different types of hearts. We always think of sowing the word to the world, which is what we all are to do once we are equipped, which seldom happens, but those having the burden of equipping the saints also sow seed when they preach, teach, or prophesy. The apostles, prophets, evangelists, pastors, and teachers are to sow the word, good seed, into the soil of believers as well as those outside the church. The believers are to sow the word into the entire world that the glory of the Lord would fill all the earth. Much effort within the church is given to building the relationship between the believer and God, so faith is preached, or, in serving the believer. Believers need to be taught to be focused on the world around them and not on their own failures. Failures and burdens are to be given to the Lord so that the race can continue. Paul wrote *"I press on toward the mark of the high calling of God in Christ Jesus"* (Phil. 3:14). Did Paul press on toward the goal carrying burdens of this life? Each believer in Christ has not only received a calling; he/she has received a high calling. A calling to be on top of the mountain above the storm and the issues of life. A calling that overcomes the storm when we find ourselves fighting against those things, or people, that would attempt to hinder us from accomplishing the goal.

Many saints have their eyes on the goal of winning the game. However, when a football team has possession of the ball their first goal is to make a first down, the second is to score a touchdown.   Within the goal of winning the game, the long range goal, there are many short range goals that must be accomplished in order to win the game and receive the prize - the gold cup. While staying focused on the final goal we must also focus on intermediate goals and be prepared for the battle we will face in this life in order to win. One of those intermediate goals is for the people of God to learn how to sow into all types of soil so that God can bring a harvest in due season. Paul said that he sowed and another watered but it is God who gives the increase (1 Cor 3:6). There are four different types of soil in the world that we must sow seed on. These same soils are brought into the church and also must be tended to by sowing seed continually in a manner fitting for growth.

There are times in a farmers work that the first planting does not sprout as he would have hoped so a second planting, or over seeding, is done so as to bring forth a more bountiful harvest. This takes more time and resources but is necessary to receive the desired result. Let us not lose heart in well doing. Let us continue to do what we are each called to do and not be disheartened by the results that we see. It is God who brings forth the harvest.

Prayer: *Lord God, I ask that You give me the ability to sow seed bountifully into this world. I know that You did not differentiate between different soils. I am to sow upon all types of soil. I ask that You give me the courage to sow seed and the ability to help it sprout and grow.*

The Weekly Word - Week 52
Perseverance

During any season many are in a time period of waiting on God to perform the promises He has made either through a dream, a vision, or a prophetic word spoken through another human vessel. Sometimes saints become anxious to see those promises come to pass because they so desire to fulfill their destiny in Christ. It is exciting to hear directions as to what God wants to accomplish through each of us and often it takes longer than hoped. The word of God informs us that God will *"render to every man according to his deeds: to those who by perseverance in doing good seek for glory and honor and immortality, eternal life"* (Rom 2:6-7). The Father promises us eternal life if we continue to do good. But we must persevere. If a person has not yet received the totality of the promise, he/she must continue to strive toward that end.

Paul, an apostle, wrote to his son Timothy explaining that he lived *"in the hope of eternal life, which God, who cannot lie, promised long ages ago"* (Tit 1:2). This promise of eternal life was made long ago and we live in hope, in expectation, of its performance in our lives if we continue to seek for glory, honor, and immortality which are found in Jesus.

This pattern also is the foundation for every promise God has made to us through a dream, a vision, or a prophetic word. First, God gives the promise, than a process of time must be accomplished until the performance of the promise comes. While this process of time proceeds the saint is learning more and more how to *" walk in Him, having been firmly rooted and now being built up in Him and established in your faith, just as you were instructed and overflowing with gratitude"* (Col 2:7). When God initially gives a dream, a vision, or a prophetic word to a person that person is seldom in the proper place spiritually, and at ti,es physically, for the promise to be performed.

In Isaiah 48:3 the LORD speaks these words, *"I declared the former things long ago and they went forth from My mouth, and I proclaimed them. Suddenly I acted, and they came to pass."* Our God is a God who performs things suddenly; but He gives us plenty of time to prepare for what He is going to do. Remember, He *"does nothing unless He reveals His secret counsel to His servants the prophets"* (Amos 3:7). When the LORD God speaks His prophets must prophesy what He has spoken and not add or subtract to what is being spoken by God. And it is imperative that we take what God says to heart whether by a dream, a vision, or a prophetic word and do what is necessary to come into the place where God will perform it in our lives. We cannot just go out to do it according to our own might but we must wait on the LORD to bring it to pass. *"But those who wait on the LORD will renew their strength; they shall mount up with wings like eagles, they shall run and not be weary, they shall walk and not faint"* (Is 40:31).

The word "wait" in Isaiah 40:31 means *"to bind together (perhaps by twisting), that is, collect; (figuratively) to expect."* This Hebrew word is also translated as gather (together), look, patiently, or tarry. Our waiting involves expectation as one has when waiting for a bus, waiting for the nurse to call you in to see the doctor, waiting for a taxi to take you to the airport, or waiting to hear of a new birth. We not only expect it to come, but we prepare for it. One would not be ready for the bus if they are not at the bus stop; they cannot get into a taxi dressed with a house robe; they won't see the doctor ½ an hour early, or even on time; and when expecting to hear of a new birth they may either be at the hospital or sitting close to the phone at home, or have their cell phone on. During the time of process preparation must be made for when God decides to perform the prophetic word, the vision, or the dream He has spoken to us.

When the Lord gives a promise, the enemy will begin to strategize in order to nullify that word to bring doubt and unbelief into the heart of the one receiving the word. But we must persevere through every persecution and affliction that is brought our way. We must fight the good fight of faith and we must proclaim "NO MORE DELAY!" We must seek the heart-throb of God and His will and His way; desiring for the glory, honor, and immortality that is brought by the Kingdom. Within the fulfillment of every word spoken to us comes the building of the Kingdom, a spiritual house, made with living stones fitly joined together, put properly in the place God wants it for the building of His house, His family, His determination.

Prayer: *Lord, by faith I take hold of every promise You gave to me by way of a dream, vision, or prophetic word. I ask, Lord, that You remind me of those promises that You have given to me that I have forgotten. Help me to have the patience, the perseverance, to passionately pursue the performance of Your promises.*

Table of Scriptures

20	John, the son of Zebedee	Apostles	Mk. 10:35-40
			Jn. 20:2
			Jn. 21:7
			Jn. 14:21, 23
			Jn. 10:17
			Heb. 5:4
21	Prophetic Visions	Visions	1 Sam. 3:1
			Prov. 29:17 - 19
			Acts 9:27
22	Servant or Son	Relationship	Psa. 116:16 - 17
			Gal. 4:3 - 7
			Heb. 2:10
			Rom. 8:18
23	Compassion	Compassion	Lk. 5:19
			Psa. 78:38
			Psa. 86:15
			Psa. 111:4
			Lk. 6:35
24	Hidden in the Days of Anger	Unity	Zeph. 2:1 - 3
			Zeph. 1:4-5
			Zeph. 1:6
			Phil. 3:9 - 11
			Zeph. 3:12
25	Selfishness	Self	Phil. 2:3 - 4
			Lk. 22:26
			Mat. 5:6
			Rev. 11:15
			Mat. 20:27 - 28
26	Jesus the Good Shepherd	Jesus	Jn. 10:1 - 16
27	The Full Commission (Part 1)	Jesus	Lk. 4:18 - 19
			Mat. 9:27 - 29
			Mat. 15:12 - 14
			Mat. 12:22
28	The Full Commission (Part 2)	Jesus	Jn. 5:30
			Jn. 7:24
			Jn. 6:36 - 40
29	Walking in Unbelief	Doubt	Mat. 17:14
			Mk. 16:17
30	Praying For Leaders (Part 1)	Prayer	1 Ti. 2:1 - 2
	1 Pet. 5:8		

			Heb. 13:23
			Acts 16:3 - 4
			Acts 20:4
			Acts 19:22
			Col.4:7 - 9
38	John Mark	Spiritual Son	1 Pet. 5:13
			Acts 12:12
			Col.4:10
			Acts 15:24, 36
			Acts 15:37 - 41
			1 Cor.4:15
39	New Authority	Apostles	Acts 4:36 - 37
			Lk. 9:3
			Acts 11:23, 26
40	Return To Repentance	Repentance	Mat. 3:2 - 3
			Mat. 3:8
			Mat. 4:7
			Ex. 29:39 - 42
			Mat. 19:18
			Mat. 6:43 - 44
			Acts 26:19 - 20
			Eph. 5:28
			Acts 26:16 - 18
41	Compassion	Compassion	1 Pet. 3:8 - 9
			Rom. 18: 16 - 17
			1 Cor. 12:25 - 26
			1 Jn. 3:17
42	Kings & Priests	Position	Rev. 1:6
			2 Chr. 1:10
			Ex. 18:13
			Rom. 8:27
			Heb. 11:13
			Rev. 8:4
43	From Shittim To Gilgal	Covenant	Mic. 6:5
			2 Pet. 2:15
			Nu. 25:1 - 2, 5
			Ex. 5:1
			Eph. 2:19 - 20
44	Crossing Over Jordan	Covenant	Jos. 5:4 - 5
			Jer. 4:4

51	Sower of Seed	Sowing	Jer. 29:13
			Acts 8:4
			Phil. 3:14
			1 Cor. 3:6
52	Perseverance	Patience	Rom. 2:6 - 7
			Tit. 1:2
			Col. 2:7
			Is. 48:3
			Am. 3:7
			Is. 40:31

BIBLIOGRAPHY

Kuhn, Terrance. *Holding Up Their Hands.* Bloomington, In.; AuthorHouse, 2009

Other Books and Training Manuals by Terrance Kuhn
Holding Up Their Hands
The Principles of the Doctrine of Christ
Spiritual Warfare I - Preparing For Battle
Spiritual Warfare II - Engaging in Battle
The Fundamentals of Prophetic Ministry

Whether you want to purchase bulk copies of
My Weekly Word Devotional
or buy another book for a friend, get it now at:
www.abooksmart.com

If you have a book that you would like to publish,
contact Jon McHatton, Publisher, at A Book's Mind:
jon@abooksmind.com.

www.abooksmind.com